JOURNEY
OF THE DREAMER

THE PATH TO DISCOVERING THE LIFE OF YOUR DREAMS

BY DONAVON ROBERSON

Table of Contents

Title Page 1
Preface 2
Introduction to Dreaming 7
Understanding the Journey of the Dreamer 33
Understanding the Outer and Inner World 38
The Four Steps to Greatness 43
Layers in the Journey of the Dreamer 50
Choose to ANSWER 57
Articulate the Dream 63
Achieve the Dream 78
Acknowledge 85
Awareness 92
Awakening 97
5 Essentials of the Extraordinary Life 103
Passion 107
Purpose 109
Practice 113
Peace 117
Begin Your Origin Story 121
Bonus Chapter: Time to Take Risks 140
Closing Thoughts 143
The Journey of the Dreamer Resource Guide: 145
About Donavon 147

The Journey of the Dreamer

A Guide to Living the Life of Your Dreams!

By Donavon Roberson
www.thejourneyofthedreamer.com

Preface

What you have in your hands is a guide. It is not a definitive work, not an academic study, not a scientific publication. It is a guide—one meant to encourage and inspire you to live into your destiny. That sounds a bit lofty. Even as I type it, I can hear the cynic in me crying out in disbelief. That may be your response as well. But my desire is that, by the end of this book, we have come to some understanding that allows for the cynic and the dreamer to lock arms and create something amazing together. I mean, really, can't we all just get along?

Remember back to when you were a kid. Seriously. Stop for a moment and think back to some of your earliest childhood memories. Who did you dream of being? Where did you want to go? What did you plan on doing? As kids, we could be anyone, we could go anywhere, we could do anything that we could imagine. Our imaginations weren't limited to budgets, timelines, or value. Our dreams were free of fear and free to roam. We could drive a submarine in the deepest caverns of the ocean one moment, and in the next we could be flying through the open skies without the need of any machinery or propulsion device. We were free. We were dreamers. We were alive.

The only limits to our dreams were those of our own imaginations! Think about it. We could be anyone, do anything, go anywhere! If we could dream it, we could do it ... and we did.

As life moved on, many of us left our childhood dreams for more measurable and more acceptable aspirations. We were convinced our dreams were unrealistic. We were instructed on what dreams were acceptable. We were encouraged to be more logical with our choices and to go the way of the culture and march to the beat of the drum of safety and security. We were told that it would the responsible thing to dive into a career while still young and plan to go after our dreams once we had made something of ourselves. And so we did. As life moved on, many of us stopped actively dreaming because we looked at people around us and realized that this world doesn't value dreamers or their dreams; instead, we value what's practical and reasonable.

I also understand that life happens. There are times when the dream seems out of our control or reach. There are times when the dream may not be easily managed or achieved. There are times when the dream is epic and seemingly impossible to bring about.

Think about the dreams you had at the end of your time of schooling. Did you still want to do and be all of those things you imagined in childhood? Did you still dream of soaring above the clouds? Did you still close your eyes only to open them and find that you were on a spaceship exploring the outer reaches of the universe? Did you still envision yourself standing in front of a classroom and encouraging young people to expand their horizons?

Some of us could see ourselves there, but for many of us ... the dream was gone. By *gone* I simply mean that we had accepted the wisdom of the ancients that had been imparted to us, to grow up and think about our future. The dream was still there, but we had put it in a box, then put that box on a shelf and decided that it was best to keep it out of arm's reach for the time being. In fact, many of us became so disconnected from our dream that we tucked other things around the dream so as to hide it away completely.

And there it sat. In a box. On a shelf. Collecting dust.

Life has a way of getting in the way. Life has a way of slipping through our fingers. Life has a way of moving on while we simply watch in disbelief. Time slips by. Minutes become hours, become days, become weeks, become years, become decades. Before we know it, we are entrenched in the process of making something of ourselves. Before we know it, we have barricaded ourselves behind responsibilities of every kind. Before we know it, our dreams are but a distant memory, and we have become a shadow of our former selves.

And so here we are. Being reminded of our childhood dreams. Being challenged to find the shelf, open the box, remove the dream, dust it off ... and become reacquainted with that which once gave us life.

What will you do? Will you do what most people do, and just accept that your dreams are something of the past, not to be thought of as possible or even valuable? Or will you dare to break free from the negative thinking that has held you back from revealing your true sense of genius ... your truest greatness?

I am praying—and begging—that you consider the latter. You have a greatness within you, and I bet that it is somehow tied to your deepest dreams. This greatness wasn't given to you so that you could put it in a box and hide it on a shelf in the recesses of your mind. This greatness was given to you so that you would make this world a better place, because you dared to tap into your own power. I believe your dreams reveal your true greatness, and that your greatness was given to you as a gift for humanity. I believe that to not go after that dream is to hold humanity back from reaching its full potential.

I know that it sounds like I am being overly dramatic, and maybe I am (to a degree). But really, what is the harm? I want to see you live into your full potential, and my guess is that you aren't doing that.

That's what this journey is all about: to help people break free from monotonous lives and to live the life of their dreams. That's my calling and my passion. I tell people this all the time, and I truly believe it: my purpose in life is to help reconnect you with your greatness. In other words, to help you become the greatest version of yourself possible.

In this book, we're going to talk about that from various standpoints, beginning with what dreaming actually is. I find that a lot of people struggle with the concept of dreaming. They don't know what dreams are; they don't know how to dream. They don't know that they can dream, or they're afraid to dream. That's often why they're stuck.

I want to take you on a journey to understand that you're able to dream; in fact, that you were designed and created to dream. All of us human beings were. Our dreams are simply an extension of our personalities and an extension of our purpose.

Introduction to Dreaming

I think our dreams are intrinsically tied to who we are as individuals. I believe our dreams have been given to us and are spiritual in nature. I believe that when we allow ourselves to dream, we tap into the divine and spiritual nature of our lives, and we have the privilege of seeing what truly is. When we dream, we experience divine moments of inspiration when we tap into eternity and see what truly is. Think about that for a moment! What if the reality we currently experience isn't reality at all? What if the life that we currently live is a shadow of the reality we were meant to live? The journey of the dreamer isn't just about having stuff—it's about becoming the best possible version of ourselves. When we dream, we tap into the divine calling on our life to do more and be more. I believe that dreaming is our future reality calling to our present to come and partake in all that can be and will be when we surrender ourselves to the dream.

Let's do a little dive into dreams—and what they are and aren't.

First, let's talk about what dreams aren't:

- They aren't simply a list of goals or tasks to complete
- They aren't a "pie in the sky" approach to life
- They aren't an ethereal list of wishes or wants that we hope to have some day

- They aren't fluffy thoughts that come and go, stirring emotion and offering hope without substance or meaning

So what, exactly, is a dream? In his book *The Dream Manager,* Matthew Kelly defines a dream as *the richly imagined future.* Let me break that down a bit: He writes about the fact that each of us lives in the *now*, that is, our own reality. Look around you and consider the life you are living right now. Now imagine that life being complete and whole and something beyond your wildest imagination. That's your richly imagined future.

The life we have now and live now is a result of choices we have made. Our richly imagined future has not yet been lived or realized, but it's something we can live into when we allow ourselves the freedom to go there and give ourselves permission to do what it takes to get there. The journey we go on between our *now* and our *richly imagined future* is the journey of the dreamer.

Another way to say this is that the *journey of the dreamer* is the process we go through to get from where we are to where we want to be—from our now, to our richly imagined future. It's how we go about changing areas in our lives that we would like to improve or discover: that is the journey of the dreamer. The dreaming process means realizing our dreams; creating our reality through dreams.

So let's talk about the anatomy of a dream. There are two aspects to a dream: cause and effect. Everything in life is about cause and effect. When we talk about dreaming, cause is that thing that we are going after; the motivation, the destination. Most people, when considering their dreams, think about things they would like to possess, or experiences they would like to have. In this phase, dreams tend to focus on the motivation of happiness. We want to be happy, and we feel that these things, these articles, will make us happy. We wish for things we believe are needed to achieve happiness, or bliss, or satisfaction. These are the *cause* elements of the dream.

So then, what are the *effect* elements of the dream? If the cause was about the article, then the effect is about attitude. Another way of stating this is that the *cause* is about the motivation and the *effect* is about the action we take. If the cause is about the destination, then the effect is about the journey. The effect is what we go through as a dreamer along the journey. It's about who we become as the dreamer. The dream changes us; it helps us become the best version of ourselves.

You see, when we start this process of a journey toward our dreams, we have a destination in mind. We begin to move in the direction of that destination, but along the way we discover that we aren't who we need to be if we are to reach the destination. So we have to change. We have to become the dreamer capable of realizing the dream.

To change your existing reality and experience your future reality, you must become a new person. The dream changes the dreamer to make you the best version of yourself possible. Think about it for a moment: If you WERE, right now, the individual that you need to be in order to have your richly imagined future, then you already would have your richly imagined future. You are NOT that person yet, but you will become that person as you take this journey.

Don't get me wrong: The elements are there. The person is there. The greatness is there. It takes the journey for us to discover who we really are and to uncover the reality that is.

Let's dive a little more into this idea of becoming a better version of yourself. Please understand that I believe you are already wonderful. You are uniquely and wonderfully made and fashioned by God.

So why should you want to become a better version of yourself? Because life is a journey. We are all in the process of discovering our greatness. We are all in the process of growing and maturing and becoming better individuals. The journey of the dreamer allows us to get there.

For many of us, it's not a stretch to look at our lives and see mistakes and failures that we want to correct. We often live life through the lens of checks and balances. We hope the good things we do outweigh the negative things in our lives. And many of us get stuck looking at the negative aspects of our lives and feel overwhelmed by the daunting task of overcoming our shortcomings. The journey of the dreamer allows us to take the focus off the past and look to the future to determine the next steps. Rather than being motivated by a need to outrun our shortcomings, mistakes and failures, we can look to the future—a richly imagined future—and move toward something beautiful. Rather than running away from our damaged lives, we have the privilege of being able to live into our dream life.

I don't know about you, but I would rather become a better version of myself by living into what could be, rather than reflect on what has been. Rather than living in a current reality shrouded in pain and regret, I can lean into and live into a richly imagined future illuminated by hope and happiness, thereby becoming the best version of me possible. To me, that is an amazing motivator, an inspiration for life. The idea of "the best version of me possible" comes from psychologist Abraham Maslow's theory of a "hierarchy of needs." It's what is meant by the term *self-actualized.* To be self-actualized means that we live in a state of flow. It means that we are all-in, in every aspect of our lives. I like to put it this way: I am a human *being,* not a human *doing.* To be self-actualized means that we are in a state where we are fully present and fully powerful.

Let's take that phrase for just a moment being and break it down. *Being* is a form of the verb *to be.* To be, in the present tense, is *I am.* Those readers with a church background will understand that *I Am* is a name for God. *I Am* means that God is present: in the past, in the present, and in the future. *I am* simply means complete and full. As beings, we are created in the image of God. I believe that means that we are human *I am*.

We are to be present in this moment. We are to be full in this moment. We are to be complete in this moment. And when we get to that place, that is when we experience self-actualization. That is the final destination of the journey of the dreamer.

What does that look like, ultimately? What do we experience when we're in that state? In other words, how do we know that we have arrived?

It's really simple. Have you ever been happy? If you have, then you have experienced a taste of this state of being. Happiness can be defined as gratification, fulfillment, contentment, delight, having found worth, satisfaction, bliss, etc. Most of us have probably experienced moments of happiness. And while I believe this to be part of the experience, I do not believe it to be the final destination. I believe the final destination, that is, the truly self-actualized person, is a place where one experiences *joy,* rather than mere happiness.

You may think this is just semantics. But I'd like to differentiate between the two. Many of us know the Serenity Prayer: "God, grant me the serenity to accept the things I cannot change, the courage to change the things I can, and the wisdom to know the difference." Most of us probably think that's the whole thing. But there is more, and the addition is beautiful! The full Serenity Prayer goes like this: "God, grant me the serenity to accept the things I cannot change, the courage to change the things I can, and the wisdom to know the difference. Living one day at a time, enjoying one moment at a time, accepting hardship as the pathway to peace. Taking, as Jesus did, this sinful world as it is, not as I would have it. Trusting that you will make all things right if I surrender to your will. That I may be reasonably happy in this life and supremely happy with you forever in the next. Amen."

I love the additional piece to this, because it acknowledges the fact that many of us have experienced hardship. Our current situation, our *now*, is not our dream, nor is it the life of our dreams. The prayer also acknowledges the difference between happiness and supreme happiness. The idea of supreme happiness is what I call joy. Joy happens when we rise above our circumstances and experience life in the moment. We experience it by being present. That is the final destination of the dream. The final destination of the dream is to experience joy.

I want to show you how to get there. I want to take this journey with you to experience joy; that is, to experience supreme happiness In life. If the final destination of the journey of the dreamer is to experience joy by adding value to life ... then an element of that is to become "whole." Remember, we already talked about being a "human *I am*," meaning one who lives in the moment and experiences the present fully and completely. To make this happen, we need to be whole and grow in every area of life. To live in wholeness, I must take care of all areas of life: body, mind and spirit. I am constantly looking to my life and evaluating what I think, feel and do. It's really simple: what I think is what I believe about life, which affects how I feel about life, which drives what I do in life—which ultimately affects what I think about life. Again, the Journey of the Dreamer is about me becoming the best version of me, on the way to achieving in life all that I dream and desire. The process of becoming whole allows me to fast-track the process and the journey and live my dream life faster.

To be "whole" means that we take into account our basic human needs through the dreaming process: physical, mental, emotional, social, financial, material and spiritual. As I work with someone to begin the journey of the dreamer, this is the place where we begin. In fact, when we get to the *Dream Storming* section of the process, this is the framework we use to start the dream list. When you keep all of these elements in mind, as you create your dream list and follow through on your dreams, you will be intentional about creating wholeness and positive wellbeing.

Now, before we jump into the journey, there is one more area to address, to ensure you have the tools needed to make your dreams a reality. And that is:

What is stopping you from becoming the "best version of me"? Why aren't you already living your richly imagined future? Why aren't you at least moving in that direction? For some, it is a question of value. Is there value in the dream? To determine value we simply need to ask the question: What is most valuable in my life?

In life there is extrinsic value and intrinsic value. Extrinsic value would be things like money, appearance or status. Intrinsic value would include things like novelty, relationships, and impact. Neither is right or wrong; they are just different ways to assign value in life. It's important to take the time to decide what happiness looks like for you, by determining what you most value in life.

I know what you are asking right now, because I have the same question sometimes: Isn't pursuing my own happiness self-serving and selfish? It's a logical question, and one we've been conditioned to ask. It's a thought we have been guilted into—and a question we need to stop asking. If the purpose of life is to be our best self, then shouldn't we experience moments of happiness along the way? If the final destination of the journey of the dreamer is to experience joy by adding value to life, then an element of that is to become "whole." To live in wholeness, we must care of all areas of life, as mentioned earlier and summarized as body, mind and spirit.

Here is my point: when you are at your best, we ALL benefit. When you are at your best, and experiencing happiness and joy, then you are unleashing your greatness on the rest of us and helping us achieve our own happiness and joy. When we awaken the dream within us, we allow other people to dream, too; we allow people to have that spark. We open them up to the possibility of greatness, so they start this journey as well. It's like the oxygen mask on an airplane: if the cabin pressure drops, adults are to take care of themselves and then care for the children near them. To be able to take care of others, we must take care of ourselves.

Having said all of that, here is something I live by when it comes to the question, "Should I live out this dream?" If the value in my dreams brings about happiness (mine or others), then go for it! The purpose of life is to enjoy life, moment-by-moment, and ultimately that takes place when we share those experiences with other people. For others, the question isn't one of value but of ability. The answer to the question of value is a resounding "yes," but we don't feel that we have what it takes to make the dream a reality. The reason is that our reference points are skewed; the lens through which we view life is distorted.

This concept of "reference points" is inspired by Tony Robbins. Simply put, we make decisions in life based on experiences we've had. These experiences teach us to respond to situations or circumstances in certain ways that ultimately influence our reality, becoming reference points on which we base our assumptions about our ability to achieve our dreams. There are three types of reference points: past, present and future. Each influences us, from the perspective of ourselves and others.

Let me give you an example. When I was a kid I had always wanted to be a fighter pilot and had dreams of going to the Air Force Academy. I had model airplanes hanging from my bedroom ceiling, I loved watching the iconic movies of my time (*Top Gun, Iron Eagle, Hot Shots*, etc.) and could visualize myself in the cockpit of an F-16, grabbing the stick and banking to the left before throttling back and rolling into a textbook evasive maneuver! It was brilliant! When I was a freshman my homeroom teacher asked me what I wanted to be and do after high school, and when I shared this with him he politely chuckled and let me know that it wasn't possible. He then went on to explain that only a handful of students from our high school had ever made it and that I didn't have "what it would take" to make the dream a reality. That statement became a reference point for me. In that moment, I believed that I wasn't qualified to go after that dream, and in that moment I questioned if I had "what it would take" to achieve any of my dreams.

While some people regard statements from others like that one as a challenge and confront such comments head-on (a response that I have taken on as my own in recent years), for me as a freshman this was a crushing statement, and it moved me in a direction away from my dreams. Many dreamers I have worked with have had similar "reference points" in life, which have created hurdles and obstacles that put space between the dreamer and their dreams.

Now that we know what a dream is, we're ready to move on toward starting the journey. I want to show you how to get there. I want to take this journey with you to experience joy; that is, to experience supreme happiness in life. And that is the purpose of this book.

I am a firm believer of "what you put into something is what you will get out of it" so I have tried to make this book easy to read and navigate through, while being very practical and action oriented. I want this to be a book that inspires you to step into your greatness and take actions that you may have never taken before. My hope is that as you read the chapters you will take notes on your observations and insights, honestly answer and interact with the Application Questions and Action Steps at the end of each chapter, interact with other dreamers on The Journey of the Dreamer Facebook Page and (more than anything) take your life to another level as you engage in this process.

I am also making a number of resources available to help along the Journey! I will attempt to share those resources throughout the book but know that I will make a complete list of each resource available at the very end of the book. Again, my desire is that this is a very hands on and practical guide to helping you reconnect with your greatest self as you engage in the process of achieving your dreams!

Becoming The Dreamer

Think back to when you were a kid. As kids, we used to dream about anything and everything. I remember playing with G.I. Joes or Star Wars figures. We would build sets. We would go out and dig holes and tunnels, and play with those action figures in the holes and the tunnels. In our imaginations we became the action figures. We'd put ourselves right in the midst of everything.

Play was part of the process of dreaming. We'd use our imaginations and become part of the storyline, one of the characters. What that did for us as kids was open up a space to dream. Tapping into our imaginations would drive us to create new worlds, to create new opportunities, to re-create ourselves in many ways. We would dream of who we wanted to be and where we wanted to be and what we wanted to do.

We would dream about it for the future, but even more important, for the present. In that moment, when I was pretending to be a superhero or a Jedi Knight, that's who I was, and you couldn't convince me otherwise. My dreams were so powerful, so real, so authentic. They were so much a part of who I was and who I wanted to be. When I think about my own kids today, we've come a long way with toys, games and movies. There's so much coming at them to keep them occupied, yet they still dream. We go out for Halloween and we get these costumes that are fantastic. It's not just a plastic face now—it's the whole nine yards.

We put on these costumes and walk around the neighborhood, and for that night, they are Wolverine or Darth Vader. What's interesting is, the magic doesn't last just for that night. My boys will keep getting out the Halloween costumes and wearing them around the house, or even when they go out. They've worn them to the gym when we drop them off for a daycare session. When they wear a costume, they believe they are that character. It's exciting for me to listen to them running around the house, making noises and imagining themselves as someone else. It's exciting for me, because they're using their imaginations, which opens up the space for dreaming.

So, what happened to us? What's happened along the way so that, as adults, we've shut that down imaginative ability? What caused us to go from a place of imagination and creativity and wonder and excitement to the mundane, stereotypical, boring lives most of us live? I think several things happened. One is that we were told that our dreams were just dreams. We were told to get our head out of the clouds. We were told we couldn't do those things. *You can't be a Jedi. You can't have superpowers. You can't change the world. You can't do this. You can't do that.*

All our lives, we've listened to those voices and we've accepted them as truth. Maybe we've even told ourselves those very things: *I can't do this. I can't do that.* The reason we tell ourselves those things is because, a) we're listening to those voices, and b) we've tried certain things and they haven't worked out, and now we associate those voices with our failed attempts and take on the belief that *I can't do this* is reality.

Another piece to this issue is that, as a society, we've put imagination and creativity and play into a realm that's for kids only. Kids are allowed to make the world of imagination their reality, but as adults we need to be responsible, grown-up, real. We need to live real lives, and those lives have become boring. We've moved into this space of accepting that creativity and imagination aren't reality, and so we've given up on our dreams.

It probably happened to you in high school. People started to tell us we were weird because of our dreams. Others thought we were weird and thought our dreams were weird, and they said so. So it made us a little self-conscious, and in our self-consciousness we decided we weren't going to move forward with our dreams, or at least we wouldn't talk about them. We still had dreams, but we weren't going to reveal them because we didn't want people to shoot us down.

Then, maybe through our college years, we tried, we ventured out toward a few of our dreams. We tried a couple of things and weren't successful, and so we decided we had to give up because it was time to get a real job or make real money, or it was time to accept reality and take responsibility. Maybe some of us didn't get a chance to dream because of choices we made that pushed the limits and didn't allow us to move into that place of imagination and creativity. Then, as adults we just kind of accepted it, that *this is it.* This is where we are. This is what our lot in life is.

I want to tell you that this is not your lot in life. If you're not dreaming, not using your imagination and not using your creativity, I want to invite you, I want to encourage you, I want to beg that you open up space for those things in your life. While once we were perhaps driven by self-consciousness, by accepting what others said about us, now we've moved into a space of fear. Now we're so disjointed and disconnected from our imagination that going into that space stirs up anxiety.

For some people, merely to think about being creative—for example, shutting yourself in a room with a pad of paper or a whiteboard and allowing your imagination to go crazy—brings up anxiety and a host of old issues. Some people wouldn't even attempt it for fear of coming up with a stupid idea. We're afraid of being disappointed, or of disappointing somebody else. We're afraid of failing, when failing sometimes is necessary. If we're going to live this life we've been given to the fullest, if we're going to re-engage with our heart and our soul and our passion and our purpose, then we have to get past that fear and step into a place of imagination and creativity.

The easiest way to begin is by simply allowing yourself to play. Get out some toys. If you have kids, get on the floor with your kids. Let them guide you through the exercise. Let them give you the tools and the resources you need to be able to use your imagination and to dream and create a new place. Sit down with them and ask questions. Drop some Legos on the floor and ask, "Okay, what are we going to build? Where do we live? What are we going to do? Who are we going to be?" Ask the questions and allow them to come up with the answers. That's the space of imagination, of play. That's where creativity happens. And that's the place where we can begin to tap into our dreams again.

Allow yourself the opportunity to play, and then the opportunity to create. Spend some time creating something. Spend some time drawing, painting, creating a recipe. Spend some time writing a book, doing arts and crafts. Spend some time where you're just creative and you allow that creativity to flow from you. Turn play into a space of creativity and creation.

The final step is to turn that creation into a space of imagination, the space of the dream. Dare to open up your mind to not what is probable, but what is possible. Dare to open your mind, to think of things that are beyond your imagination right now. You don't have to come up with an answer for how to do it. You simply have to come up with a destination, a desired outcome. You simply have to imagine something that's so impossible that it becomes possible. That is how you become a dreamer.

Now is the time to focus on Beliefs and Behaviors:

Application Questions:
- What were some of your childhood dreams?
- When did you put your dreams in a box and hide them away on a shelf?
- What would you like to create but you're too afraid to make it happen?

Action Items:
- Dare to Play: spend some time coloring, playing with some clay or drawing
- Whiteboard: draw out a crazy idea that you have but haven't worked on
- Imagination time: spend 10 minutes a day for the next week using your imagination or some time staring at the clouds imaging what you see

Declutter Your Life

What's the next step in becoming a dreamer? Now that you've opened up this space of creativity and imagination, you've opened yourself to what's possible. The idea is to tap into the dreams already in your head and heart. Maybe you've had a particular dream for a long time but you've put it into a box on a shelf, and you've put stuff in front of it and basically forgotten that it's there.

Every once in a while, we might hear a message, we might hear a speech, we might see a movie, we might have a conversation with somebody that stirs our heart and connects us with that dream. Maybe you think about that dream, but the thought of failing at it is so real and raw that you dare not entertain the dream anymore, and so you put it back up on that shelf and leave it alone. Some of us, when that stirring happens within us, walk over to the closet, move some of the things away and look at the box.

We remember what it felt like to dream, and to be connected to that dream. But because of fear and self-doubt, we feel we're not worthy of it. We cover the dream back up and walk away. Some, when they get that stirring in their heart, walk into the closet, move things aside, grab the box, open the box, and look at the dream again. They wonder and ponder and begin to imagine once again what it would be like to make that dream come true. Again, because of fear and trepidation, they shut the box and, with a heavy heart, put it back on the shelf and cover the box back up.

My desire for you is that you walk into that closet and look at every shelf that has a dream covered by stuff, and you begin to move the clutter out of the way so that you can get to those dreams. How do you get rid of it, so that you can re-attach yourself to the dream?

First, recognize where the clutter is coming from. For many of us, the clutter is in our own minds; it's clutter other people have put there. In our heads, we play records from our past over and over again, in which people said: *You can't do that. You're not worth it. You're not good enough for that. You're never going to make this happen.* What happens is that those words get etched into our minds and hearts, creating a groove like those in an old vinyl record as we continue to entertain them. As we begin to think about these dreams, that record begins to play, and those words become real as they play in our minds over and over and over again.

I want you to take some time right now to write down some of those words—those records, distractions, detractors from your dreams—that are keeping you from becoming the greatest version of yourself. What are those voices saying to you? Write it down. For some of us, this may take a long time. There may be lots of paper involved, and that's okay. Get those things out.

As you're doing this, please understand that I don't want you to interact with those words, whether they're true or not. I simply want you to write down what you hear, what you tell yourself, what you allow others to tell yourself. The reality is that much of what you're going to write down is not true. It's a story somebody has created. It's a story you have created about what others have said or about what you have said.

These words are the objects that are hiding your dreams at the back of the closet and keeping you from dreaming. These words are the objects you have used to shield you and to keep you from your dreams. It's time to declutter that closet. The best way to get those things out of the way is to acknowledge their presence by writing them down.

Once you've written all those things down on paper, look at each one and ask yourself—truly ask yourself: *Is this true about me? Is it true that I'm not worthy? Is it true that I'm incapable? Is it true that I'll never be able to make these things happen? Is it true that I'll always be this way? Is it true that I'm a failure?* If we're honest with ourselves, for many of us the first instinct is to say, "Yeah, that's true," because it's a story that we've told ourselves for along time.

But the truth is this: If you can dream it, you can do it. If you can dream it, you deserve it. Remember what I said earlier. Your dreams are directly tied to your person and to your purpose. Your dreams are unique to who you are. They're unique to who you are because they're part of who you were created to be, who you were designed to be. My belief is, if you dream it and you can do it and you deserve it, then all of these stories that you're telling yourself right now aren't real. They're not true. You can do anything you set your mind to do; you simply have to become the person who can do it. That's what we're going to talk about. That's the journey we're on.

Next, we're going to take these records that you've written down and break them, flip them and turn them around. Get a fresh sheet of paper for this. We're going to take each of these negative statements that have plagued you for years, turn them around and make them positive. What we have told ourselves for years has kept us from dreaming. It hasn't helped us become the greatest versions of ourselves. It won't get us where we want to be. It won't help us become the people we want to become.

It's time to turn those statements around so they do help us. For instance, if you wrote down "I'm not worthy," we're going to flip that statement around and write on this new sheet of paper: "I'm absolutely worthy." Notice I added *absolutely*. Here's why: for some of us, just writing down *I am worthy* is a stretch, but if you write down "I'm *absolutely* worthy," you'll need to own it, believe it, and accept that that's the reality of your life. That is truth. What you *don't* deserve and what you're *not* worthy of is the life you've been living up to this point, if it's substandard, subpar, unfulfilling. A life in which you have beaten yourself up time and time again because you've believed the lie that you're not worthy.

Another example. If you've written down "I'll never make a change, I'll never amount to anything," I want you to flip that around: "I will amount to something. I will absolutely amount to something. I will absolutely amount to everything in life."

Do you see what I did there? Changing the records, the statements, means you're making a decision to change your own negative beliefs. By flipping the records from a negative to a positive statement, you're breaking those old habits of thought. I believe that our actions are driven by what we believe. Our beliefs are driven by the words we use. If we use words that are negative, then we believe those negative things in our lives. If we believe there are negative things in our lives, then we act in a way that supports the belief.

The quickest way to change our behaviors is to change our words. When we change our words, we change our core beliefs about who we are. The next time the thought *I'm not worthy* comes to you, stop and say to yourself, *You know what? I'm absolutely worthy, and I'm going to make this happen.*

Now that we've acknowledged all of those statements, those bits of clutter in your mental closet, we're going to declutter it. We'll flip the records and break their power over us.

Take that paper on which you wrote all those negative statements and destroy it: rip it, shred it, burn it—whatever you have to do. Destroy the old negative records that kept you from your dreams. Take the new sheet of paper with the positive statements and make it your manifesto. This is your heart's cry. I want you to read it, ponder it, interact with it.

When you interacted with the negative statements in the past, my guess is that there was negativity, pain and darkness involved with that. Now look at the positive records, the positive statements. My desire is that as you read them, your emotions are stirred. You may find that just reading these positive statements may be hard the first couple of times, because for so long you've bought into the lie that these are not true.

I want you to buy into the reality that these statements *are* true. These statements are real. This is your heart's cry. This is your desire. This is your reason for living and for being. I want you to read these statements and post them somewhere you can read them every day, twice a day. Read them until they become such a part of who you are that you can repeat them over and over and over from memory. That's going to be huge, because that in itself is going to allow you to declutter, to remove the crap from your mental closet and allow you to tap into your dreams again.

Remove the clutter. Declutter the closet, get rid of those statements that have been holding you back. Develop statements that recreate your belief in yourself and in your ability to achieve. When you have done that, we'll be able to talk about your dreams and how to actually make those dreams happen.

Now is the time to focus on Beliefs and Behaviors:

Application Questions:
- What clutter is keeping you from dreaming?
- What are you missing out on by allowing the clutter to keep you from your dreams?
- What is the false belief that you have claimed about yourself because of the clutter?

Action Items:
- What movies, books, stories or shows stir up something deep within you? Make a list of the movie, the emotion and then determine the meaning.
[visit www.thejourneyofthedreamer.com/worksheets for a worksheet]

- Create a Clutter List
  - Write down all of the words or beliefs that keep you from dreaming
  - On another paper flip the statements into positive belief statements
  - Destroy the old beliefs and adopt the new beliefs!

Understanding the Journey of the Dreamer

Until now I've been talking about the journey of the dreamer. But really what we're talking about is the journey of the *doer*. Some people may be willing to dream, but get stuck at the point of doing. They're just not willing to do the things they need to do to achieve the dream. And so being stuck becomes a self-fulfilling prophecy. These people find themselves living a life that is uneventful and unfulfilling, so they start looking to distractions to avoid dealing with it. Addictions and depression often enter the picture. A lot of times, people are stuck in a rut and don't even know it, or if they're aware of it they don't know how to get out of it.

Joseph Campbell describes the doer as part of his concept of the Hero's Journey.

Campbell, in essence, describes the Hero's Journey as beginning with normal life. The would-be hero is just putzing around, doing his thing or her thing, living an Ordinary Life, oblivious to what's going on around because he knows what he knows; she knows what she's comfortable with.

This is our comfort zone, the place where we get stuck. Then, all of a sudden, a mentor comes along and challenges the hero, prodding him or her to go forward and discover greatness.

I want to be that mentor, that sage that comes alongside you and says, "Listen, there's more to life than just normal. There's more to life than what you've been living and what you're stuck in."

The mentor pushes and prods and gets us to take a step into a different world, one where there will be journeys and challenges and trials. In this other world, there will be friends and companions who will come alongside and help make your journey a reality.

In Campbell's explanation of the Hero's Journey, there comes a point when he talks about the death of the hero. This is when you reach a place when you are staring into the Abyss: the point where you actually get to the bottom of who you are, what you're about, and what's been holding you back. The Abyss is very dark and lonely; it's a place where you must defeat the demons, the devil, the monster, whatever it is that's holding you back and keeping you from becoming your greatest self.

After that challenge, that death, takes place, a new life springs forth. You come out of that Abyss a new person, with a new life, a new calling, a new passion, a new desire. When you come out of that, living as a hero in that underworld, there are triumphant victories and battles where you can't be defeated because of what you've learned and what you've gone through.

You take that triumph over the worst back into your everyday reality. You go back into the real world with that experience, creating a new normal. There will be challenges along the way, but you will rely upon what you learned in the other world. Now you're the hero. You come back and you create a new norm, not only for yourself but for other people.

I believe that the journey of the dreamer means unpacking that entire story and becoming the hero of your own journey. (I've created a model that we'll walk through that will help to make that happen, see Figure 1.)

Then, it's about becoming the *doer*. How do we learn about this journey and make it something that we can actualize? We need to truly live out the journey so that our dreams don't simply live in our minds and hearts and fantasies, but rather become something so real, something we're so tapped into, that we know exactly what we need to do and who we need to become to make the dream a reality. That's the journey of the dreamer.

I'm excited to walk with you on this journey. I'm excited most of all because of the person you're going to become: the greatest possible version of yourself. Thank you for allowing me the opportunity. So let's start out on this journey: the journey of the dreamer.

Now is the time to focus on Beliefs and Behaviors:

Application Questions:
- What dreams have you been thinking about going after but you haven't taken action on?
- What action could you take today to help you start the Journey? When will you take that action?
- Describe your "extraordinary life". What would it feel like to make that a reality?
  Who do you need to become in order to make it happen?

Action Items:
- Check out the Journey of the Dreamer Visual and interact with it:
  Where are you on the Journey? What are the next steps for you on the Journey?
  [visit www.thejourneyofthedreamer.com/worksheets for a printable copy of the Visual]
- Visualize your Extraordinary Life: in a journal, write as many details as possible. Be Specific!
- Create a vision board of your Extraordinary Life! Keep it visible and dream over it regularly!

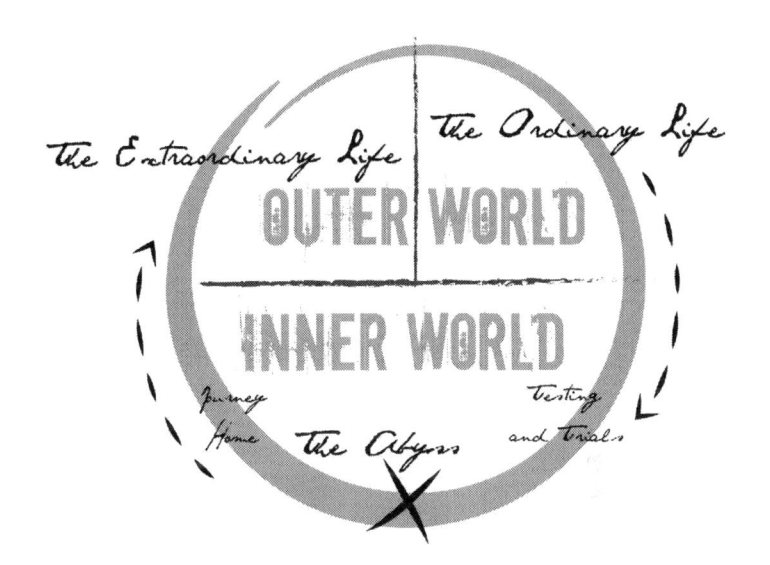

Figure 1

Understanding the Outer and Inner World

Along the Hero's Journey, there are three worlds.

The first world we find ourselves in is the Outer World. It is our ordinary day-to-day life, where we interact with everybody in the usual manner. It's where we're entrenched in our comfort zones, in the status quo. Every epic tale begins here: with Ordinary Life.

The second world is a special realm—an Underworld, if you want to call it that. I think of this special place as the Inner World. To become the hero of our own journey, we have to be willing to move into this Inner World, this special place of training and trial. In the Inner World we may face testing and tribulation and failure; to pass through places where we trip and places where we stumble. We're not alone when we're in this place. On this journey, we have a mentor, a guide, a sage, somebody who is journeying with us, walking with us, helping us along the way.

I want to come alongside of you in your own Hero's Journey and be your sage. I want to journey with you. I want to be there with you when you stumble and fail, when you make mistakes—because we need somebody with us to let us know that it's okay, to help get us back up on our feet, to dust us off, and to move us on again; and to make sure that we learn from the process.

The step you must take to get from the Outer World, the Ordinary Life, into the Inner World, into that special life where the training and trials and tribulations come, involves responding to *a call to action*. There's a call to action where the sage steps in.

The dream coach steps in and says, "Listen, there's more to life than your current reality. There's more to life than the Ordinary Life. There's more to life than the familiar day-to-day living that you're used to." I'm calling you to take action—to do something, to step out in faith, to step out in strength, to step out in confidence and do something with your life, to do something because you know, deep within you, with every fiber of your being, that something is calling you to greater things. Something is calling you to greatness. Something is calling you to step out. You feel it, you sense it, and you know it. You just need that push.

Inside the Inner World is a space we call the Abyss. As previously discussed, this is where the old *you* must die. In the Abyss you are challenged and tested, and you ultimately return feeling more bold, more powerful, and stronger than you could ever have imagined. Now you embrace the adventure, and you journey out of the special world back to the Outer World.

You take what you learned as you rose from the Abyss, and you apply it. You defeat those fears and anxieties, and those voices in your head that held you back. You put to rest all of those negative things you once held on to. You're able to test what you know now to be true and you prove that, in fact, it is true. You've conquered the Abyss, and you take your new strength, power, confidence, and skills, everything you've learned, and apply it in a fresh new way. You embrace the adventure as you step back into the Outer World, but instead of stepping back into your Ordinary Life, you step into an Extraordinary Life. You take everything you've learned and discovered, everything that you've become, and apply it to what now becomes an Extraordinary Life, an extraordinary place. A place where around every corner is a new beginning, a new challenge. You're seeing this world through new eyes, in a new light. You're seeing this world as a new you, the greatest version of you that there is. Now you begin to experience life as an Extraordinary Life, taking everything in.

Then, there's the final step, which is daring to be amazed. Dare to be amazed and to set yourself up for success, to not stay stuck in the status quo. Because the tendency will be, with time, for your new Extraordinary Life to seem ordinary again. I want you to dare to be amazed, and astonished, and astounded by life, and to go through the process again.

This process of becoming the hero of your own journey won't happen just once. Your first time through, your Abyss may not really be your deepest, darkest place. It may simply involve overcoming something that's had a grip on your life for a long time. You go to that place and you find strength and release, and you move on. Then, you go through it again, and you go through it again, and you go through it again. My friends, that is the journey of the dreamer. If we can get into the pattern and habit of doing this consistently, we will make the absolute most out of life. We will become the greatest versions of ourselves. We will know what it is to live and to engage in life in the way it was meant to be lived, and in a way we were meant to engage.

The journey of a dreamer is not a one-time event. It's a lifetime process, a process of leaving behind the Ordinary Life in the outer world to be called into action by a sage, someone who's speaking truth into your life. To be willing to take that action, to go into a new place of learning, of growth, of challenge, and trial, and risk. To die to yourself. To come out again and to apply what you've learned, to embrace the adventure, and to move into an Extraordinary Life.

Next, let's consider four steps that need to take place along this journey.

Now is the time to focus on Beliefs and Behaviors:

Application Questions:
- Does your day-to day life align with the life of your dreams?
- What does the call to "something greater" sound like to you? You may need to get quiet to hear it and spend some time with it!
- What steps in the way and keeps you from taking action? What distractions keep you stuck in the mundane aspects of life?

Action Items:
- Track your daily activities to see if you are working on your dreams OR the dreams of others?
  [visit www.thejourneyofthedreamer.com/worksheets for a tracking sheet]
- Write out a description of the "greater self" with you! Who do you need to become to make this a reality?
- Take 1 Action today to move closer toward your greatest self and your extraordinary life!

The Four Steps to Greatness

Now that we have differentiated between the outer world and the Inner World, I want to talk about the process of how we transition from, into, and through each of these. Remember, the outer world is the external one in which we live, the one everybody sees. The Inner World is that inner sanctum, that secret place, that special existence where we learn, grow, are challenged and strengthened, the place where we die to ourselves and become a greater version of ourselves than ever before.

But how we transition between these worlds is key. We need a sage, a mentor, a guide to take us into that Inner World.

The reason this is so important is that we get comfortable and complacent in our ordinary lives. Though we may hear whispers of something greater, fear and complacency and our desire to maintain creature comforts may compel us to ignore those whispers. We imagine that there is something out there for great adventurers, but that description doesn't apply to *us*. That's where a mentor steps into your life and says: "You know what? There's something greater. You're called for something greater. Let me take you there." Please don't fall into the trap of mediocrity.

When I was in high school, I had a teacher named Bill Firey. He had these sayings that we dubbed Firey-isms. One was: "Never settle for mediocrity." He meant, never settle for the status quo; never settle for good when great is out there on the horizon. Jim Collins talks about this in *Good to Great,* where he says, "Good is the enemy of great." Many of us probably would admit to having a good life, and I'm not saying that's insignificant. But don't settle for good when great is within reach. Don't settle for ordinary when extraordinary is out there, and all it's going to take is for you to step across that line and to move into that Inner World, where you will be changed and transformed and made anew.

The sage is calling you. The sage is whispering in your ear. In fact, the sage is crying out to step into action and to try something new. To take a risk. To be willing to fail and see what happens.

It reminds me of two different images that I absolutely love. First, in the Bible there is the passage that speaks of John the Baptist crying out in the wilderness, proclaiming that the Messiah is coming. That's the role of the sage in your life, to cry out in the wilderness and proclaim that greatness is on the horizon. Greatness is here. You simply need to take that step and recognize it.

Another image is that of *Indiana Jones and the Last Crusade,* when they're searching for the Holy Grail and Indiana has to take a step of faith. He's on a precipice. He can't see the way, but he knows that a leap from the lion's mouth will get him to where he needs to be; so, with fear gripping his heart as he grabs hold of his chest, he extends his foot and steps out—and lands on solid ground, because there's a bridge to take him to where he needs to be. As your dream coach (mentor, sage, etc.), I'm calling you to take that first step, to risk stepping out in faith, and trust my words that greatness is on the other side.

I understand it's risky and you're afraid. But believe me when I say that the greatness that's out there is more pleasurable than the pain that's holding you back and keeping you in your Ordinary Life. As you step into action and enter this new life, you're going to take risks and try new things. You'll succeed and you'll fail. You'll trip and you'll fall. You'll try to stand, and things will happen that will shake you at your core, and that's okay.

The next step of the journey is Conquering the Abyss. As you go through the journey of the dreamer, everything you know, believe, and feel in your core will be tested and tried, and there will come a point when you'll have to put everything on the line for something new. Think about every hero's journey you've ever heard of; every movie, every book, every adventure. There comes a time where the hero must face himself or herself, must conquer his demons, must die to herself, and must rise again.

All of us, if we're honest with ourselves, long for that to take place within us. We're tired of living the mundane life, of accepting the status quo. That's why you stepped into action. That's why you dared to take risks, dared to move into a new place—and believe me, this part is difficult. This may be the hardest thing you've faced in your life, but it will also be the most rewarding and most powerful moment in your life, when you're willing to risk it all, when you're willing to die to yourself, when you're willing to die to the things that you value most, and let go in order to attain the greatness that's waiting for you.

Conquer the Abyss. Conquer your deepest fears. Conquer the anxieties, the voices in your head that are holding you back and keeping you from excelling, that are keeping you from becoming the best version of yourself, that are keeping you from living the life you were meant to live. As you conquer the Abyss, you'll walk through a series of triumphs and victories and find a new strength and a new light and a new manner. With a new power, new purpose, and new intensity, you will experience life like you have never experienced before. You will become the master of your own destiny and of your own life. You will become the captain.

As you begin to do that, the third step is to embrace the adventure and all that you've learned, to embrace all that you've discovered: the power, the strength, the confidence that's within you to overcome your demons, to overcome your hurdles, to overcome your obstacles, to overcome all of those things that have been holding you back and keeping you at bay. The fourth step will be to step back out of this Inner World into the outer world, and you will experience an Extraordinary Life, the life that's been calling you, a life you knew existed, but didn't know how to reach. Because of everything you learned inside the Inner World, you will be able to step out into the outer world and experience an Extraordinary Life.

This Extraordinary Life will be one you have previously only imagined. But as you live this Extraordinary Life for some time, you will now accept it as your new norm. The temptation will be to settle into this Extraordinary Life as you once settled into your Ordinary Life. The temptation will be to get comfortable, become complacent, to get used to the way things are. Then things become ordinary again, which leads us to our fourth turning point: to live with abandon! To live with abandon means you understand what the journey was and that you are being called again to accept and embrace it, and to take this journey again and again and again.

You'll not accept the status quo anymore. You'll not settle for mediocrity anymore. You'll not settle into a place where the extraordinary has become the ordinary. You'll not settle into a place of comfort and complacency. You will embrace and live with abandon, giving yourself to this journey, claiming the role of the hero and continuing to press on, to press forward, to move and to grow and to embrace the greatness within you, and to continually, day by day, become the greatest version of yourself.

That is the hero's journey. Those are the turning points. Now let's get into the crux of it, and discover how we journey through the Inner World and the outer world, making the most of these twists and turns along the way.

Now is the time to focus on Beliefs and Behaviors:

Application Questions:
- How have you settled for the mundane, mediocre life?
  How does it really feel?
- Who is calling you to something greater? Who needs you to show up as your greater self?
- What is a deep fear or anxiety that you must overcome on this journey?

Action Items:
- Interact with the Four Steps to Greatness:
  - Answer the Call
  - Conquer the Abyss
  - Embrace the Adventure
  - Experience the Extraordinary
- Questions to Consider:
  - Which Step are you on right now?
  - What do you need to do next?
  - Who can help you along the Journey?

[visit www.thejourneyofthedreamer.com/worksheets for a Four Steps to Greatness Grid]

Layers in the Journey of the Dreamer

There are several layers to the journey of the dreamer. I'll outline them first and then go into much more detail in the following chapters. At the very heart of the journey are three things we need to do.

First, we need to *articulate* the dream—to state what we want. Second, we need to *architect* the dream—we need to come up with a plan for how we will make the dream a reality. And third, we need to *achieve* the dream, which means taking action.

These three things are what we do externally. But remember that the dream is something that lives within us, something we were born with, which was planted inside us from the very moment we were created, which grows and develops over time. The dream is as much a part of who we are as our personalities, gifts, talents and abilities. The dream is a true reflection of ourselves, and by grabbing hold of these initial three steps, we begin the process of making the dream that is inside us a reality to ourselves, to others, and to the world!

The next layer of the dream process happens *internally*. Things need to happen internally for us to work it out externally. We need to inwardly *acknowledge* the dream, let it *awaken* within us, and develop an *awareness* of it in our mind and heart and being. I'll go into more detail later, but for now let me explain this in the most basic way.

To acknowledge the dream simply means being honest with myself that this is something I want. Often, people have a dream they think about, consider, desire—but struggle with truly acknowledging that they want to see happen. Often, they're afraid they won't be able to accomplish the dream, or that it's simply unreasonable or unrealistic. By just *acknowledging* the dream, we begin to make it more realistic and more attainable.

Awakening happens after I acknowledge the dream and it becomes real to my mind and my heart and my soul. Awakening happens when I sit with the dream for a while and meditate on it and allow it to become real—something that I accept as my future. Awakening is simply the process of my mind and heart opening up to the possibility of the dream becoming a reality. Awakening happens when I understand that I do have the ability to achieve my dream. Awakening happens when I begin to believe the dream is attainable and is something that I am worthy of achieving. Once I acknowledge the dream and its reality in my life, and my heart has been awakened to my ability to achieve the dream, then my mind and soul become aware of the elements of the dream around me.

"Architecting" the dream is coming up with a plan for how to make the dream a reality. It's taking the time to think out a process, a set of action steps that you'll need to take to achieve the dream. Awareness happens when you begin to open your eyes to circumstances, events, people and situations and elements of the dream that have come into your life which will allow you to achieve the dream. We'll dive into these in greater detail later, but for now let's move to the next layer of the journey.

If the first layer is what we do externally, and the second layer is what happens to us internally, then this layer opens up for us in terms of feelings; it is what happens to us emotionally. A good way to sum it up is: *pleasure, passion, purpose, practice*, and *peace*.

Let's talk about each of these. As I embark on this journey of the dreamer, and begin the process of moving the dream from my head and heart to my hands and feet, I begin to experience things emotionally, because I am moving into action. The first emotion I experience is *pleasure*. I enjoy doing things that allow me to achieve the dream, because I have finally moved from something that is surreal and abstract into something very real and concrete.

The next emotion that I experience is *passion*. Passion is different from pleasure; pleasure refers to things that I *like* to do, while passion is centered around the things I *must* do. I realize that not only do I enjoy doing things that help me achieve my dreams, but they're so deeply ingrained in who I am and what I'm about that doing them gives a huge lift to my own energy, and this becomes a driving force behind all that I'm doing. Passion takes it one step further, when I realize my passion is tied not only to things that I *must* do but the things I'm *called* to do.

The next emotion is *purpose*. It's an understanding that I am here for a reason and by design; that my dream isn't just an arbitrary thought that seems to have stuck with me all of my life, but something that's been implanted in me and in my DNA from the very beginning of my existence. In other words, my dream is tied to who I am and why I am here.

Now that I understand my purpose and its place in achieving my dreams, there comes a time when I have to *practice* these steps. Malcolm Gladwell, in his book *Outliers,* talks about this principle. Those our society considers great did not become so because they were born that way but because they devoted time and effort and energy to becoming that way. Once I understand that my dream is tied to my pleasure, passions and purpose, then it becomes something that I willingly practice and work at daily, in order to experience fulfillment and joy and satisfaction in life. This practice, this work and effort we put into the process, isn't something we abhor but something we enjoy and can't live without.

The final phase we experience is that of *peace*. When we have come to a point where we are practicing our dreams, meaning that we are consistently doing things that will allow us to achieve our dreams, we find ourselves in the zone, in a space of what Maslow calls self-actualization. In its purest form, that term simply means we have arrived at the best version of ourselves. I believe that when we find ourselves in that place, we experience peace.

The journey of the dreamer is simply this: to experience these three layers in our lives in order to achieve our dreams, to make active that which lives within us. Not only will we have accomplished something externally, but internally we will have become who we were created and intended to be. The journey of the dreamer is not simply perfecting project management in our lives; it is the journey to becoming a whole person. It's the journey in which each of us is called to be the hero. It's the journey for which we were created and designed, but still often avoid and, in so doing, live a life that is less than we were meant to live.

I'm excited to walk with you through each of these stages as you learn to tap into the greatness you were born to achieve, so that you can unleash it on this world and leave humanity in a better place than it was. I believe in your greatness. I believe you have the ability to change your own world and in so doing to change the greater world. I believe that change will come as you tap into your dreams and see your dreams become a reality.

Are you with me? Are you ready to take this journey with me? Are you ready to shake off the shackles and the chains that have held you bondage for so long, in order to become the best version of yourself possible—so that you might make a difference in the lives of others and in our world? Let's do this thing together!

Now is the time to focus on Beliefs and Behaviors:

Application Questions:
- Have you thought about "who you will become" through the dream process OR have you been focused on "what you do"? Why does the "who" matter?
- How do your dreams reflect who you are at the core?
- What dream have you not acknowledged in a while? Why not start today?

Action Items:
- Engage with each Layer in the Journey of the Dreamer
  - External Layer: Articulate. Architect. Achieve.
  - Internal Layer: Acknowledge. Awareness. Awakening.
  - Emotional Layer: Pleasure. Passion. Purpose. Practice. Peace.
- Questions to Consider:
  - Where are you on the Journey?
  - Which elements excite you?
  - Which elements frighten you?

[visit www.thejourneyofthedreamer.com/worksheets for a worksheet]

Choose to ANSWER

You have been wrestling with your dream life most of your life. There has been something nagging at you, stirring in your heart, and possibly keeping you up at night.

Your dream life is calling to you. Will you answer?

To do so, you must simply make the choice. You must choose to answer the calling on your life; nobody can make that choice for you. I have intentionally used the word *choose* and not *decide*. A decision is typically the result of two options that have been presented to us, and we decide for one over the other, based on several criteria or reasons. The problem with *decisions* is that, if things don't go the way we expected, we can play the victim as a result of being "forced" into an undesired outcome. A choice, on the other hand, is not based on any particular criteria but simply on my power to choose.

I am challenging you to choose to answer the call of your dreams on your life...and make a choice to live the life of your dreams!

To **ANSWER** the calling of your dreams is to choose:

Awareness: Being aware of your surroundings means you are paying attention to every opportunity that presents itself and acting on those that move you in the direction of your dreams. We are presented with opportunities every day. The challenge is to distinguish the great opportunities from the good opportunities and embrace the great opportunities. Awareness happens when we live with eyes wide open and remain present...which leads us to the next choice we must make.

Now: To choose "now" has several implications. First, to choose *now*, means that right now, in this moment, I choose. It's easy to push off making a choice to change until some unspecified point when all our ducks are in a row. But that only leads to regret and inaction. In the same way, if we have made the choice before and find ourselves stuck and inactive, then we need to stop, accept the reality that we've gotten stuck, and actively choose to begin again. Choosing *now* also means focusing on the present. It's about using this moment as a reference point in life. We tend to get stuck in the past or paralyzed by the prospect of our future. But we need to live in the now and make the choice now...which leads to yet another choice we must make.

Sincerity: To choose sincerity means I am straightforward and honest with myself about the progress I am making. It means that I give myself permission to move forward and not worry about the end results. In a way, this is the difference between goals and outcomes: a goal is something I achieve or don't, based on a specific set of measurables that I set forth, while an outcome is something that I will always achieve as a result of effort. The challenge of outcomes is that I am moving towards something and learning along the way; the focus is on the impact of the journey and not just the destination. Being sincere means that I am happy with the progress I have made as a result of honest effort and that I learn from every experience along the way ... and yes, you guessed it: that leads to the next choice we must make.

Wonder: To choose wonder means that I choose to live with my heart wide open and take every experience and circumstance as an opportunity to learn something new. Often we approach dreams with limits and boundaries in our heads, based on past experience. What if there is something we don't know that could open up the reality of our dreams in ways you could never have imagined? To live in wonder is to approach life with the heart of a child, taking it all in and asking questions for the sake of discovering all that there is in this big, amazing world.

Excitement: Choosing excitement is to direct an emotional response that happens within us, harnessing the energy of the choice to propel us forward. Emotions are chemical reactions taking place inside us. Fear and excitement stem from the same chemical reaction, and it is our choice that determines whether it is manifested as fear or excitement. If we lean away from the opportunity that stirs up the chemical reaction within us, then we experience fear. However if we lean into the opportunity that stirs up that chemical reaction within us, then we experience excitement. Let me show you what I mean…

When I was in college I wanted "the best summer job I could imagine." My college had a summer camping program that consisted of your typical summer camp and an "extreme sports" option that included white-water rafting, rock climbing/rappelling, a high ropes course, spelunking and so much more! To participate as a facilitator in this option, I had to be trained and be prepared to be a guide in every sport for the time the group was with us. I couldn't wait to become a white-water rafting guide and spend my days floating down the New River with new groups every week…but to do that, I also had to overcome my fear of heights and tight spaces. When it came time to train for the spelunking and rock climbing/rappelling I had a choice: lean away from the feeling and allow the fear to keep me from what I truly wanted to do, OR accept the emotion, lean into it and have the summer job of my dreams. I am happy to say that I held that job for three summers and it was one of the most amazing times of my life!

To really answer the call and move into our dream life, we must harness the energy of excitement ... which leads to the final choice we must make.

Reality: To choose reality means that we choose to focus on what is real and not what isn't real. Often we look at missed opportunities, or the pain or shame brought on by our past mistakes, and interpret them as painful experiences, because we "failed." The picture of reality we create is that failure is painful — and to be avoided at all costs. Life is a journey, which means life is about progress, not perfection. We tend to mentally turn our interpretations into reality, when in fact they are simply one way to look at what we've experienced. An interpretation is a subjective conclusion based on particular reference points. I challenge you to look at these mistakes and missed opportunities through a different set of reference points, and perhaps come up with a different interpretation. Viewing a situation from different points of view moves us closer to reality ... which moves us closer to the dream life!

Are you ready to answer the call? I dare you to choose to ANSWER it today!

Now is the time to focus on Beliefs and Behaviors:

Application Questions:
- You have a choice: ANSWER the call of your dreams or don't.
  Which choice do you make most? Why?
- Which element of ANSWER resonates most with you and why? Which stretches you and why?

- How can you ANSWER the call to your dream life today?

Action Items:
- Journal this week on the ANSWER

    A: spend time looking at your surroundings and opportunities

    N: choose now: focus on this moment and all that it has for you

    S: make an honest list of all that you have done in life to be extraordinary

    W: learn something new this week [something that you've always wanted to do but haven't taken action before now]

    E: find something that frightens you – now shift the energy in your heart and mind and turn it into something you can be excited about (responsibly of course)

    R: flip your failures into positive reference points toward success

Articulate the Dream

On the Journey of the Dreamer, the first step is to articulate the dream. A dream is usually something that comes to mind now and then but isn't always top of mind, nor something you routinely act upon. Our dreams are typically always present but not very clear. Articulating the dream for yourself is important; in fact, it's the key to success.

Here's what I mean: If a dream is something you simply think about, but not really something that's regularly on your mind, something you talk about, that suggests you're not really convinced it could happen. If it's not something that moves us to take action, than the reality of it coming to life is really slim. Articulating the dream is the key to actually living out the dream, because it's what motivates action.

I hope that you understand the importance of this. When you articulate the dream you're actually giving feet to the dream. You're giving the dream power. You're declaring that the dream is important enough to you to do something about it. Essentially what you're saying is that the dream is important enough that you're willing to give it a voice.

Now I want you to think about your dream, or dreams, for a moment. This may come easily to you, or it may be extremely difficult. Wherever you find yourself, I want you to think about your dream. How would you describe it? How would you define having accomplished your dream?

If this is difficult for you, let's try a little exercise. We're going to dreamstorm. Dreamstorming is simply making a list of your dreams. To make this happen you'll need to do a few things:

1. Get a dream journal. Don't get bogged down with getting just the right fancy journal for this. You simply need a notebook or something where you can write down your dreams; something that you can take with you along this journey.

2. Set aside some time to make this happen. Dreamstorming is not something you want to rush nor is it something you want to do in a series of time blocks. This will work best if you can devote a few hours of your time to sit down and do this in one session. That isn't to say you can't come back to it and work on it several times, but the initial dream storm session should take place in one sitting.

3. Bring an open mind. That may sound ridiculously simple, as though it should go unsaid, but the truth is people sometimes struggle with the concept of dreamstorming because they come to it with a closed mind. You may be more familiar with the term "brainstorming." When I conduct a brainstorming session, there is only one rule: there are no right or wrong answers. The possibilities are endless, and the whole idea is to think outside the box. In fact I will shut down any negative conversation or comment that is made in a brainstorming session. Its purpose is

to get outside yourself and to think of solutions that are not your typical go-to answers.

The same is true for dreamstorming. A dreamstorming session is your opportunity to create space for endless possibility. This is not a goal-setting session, although we will use and apply goal-setting principles to the action plan. This is a dream list—a wish list, of sorts. Think about it this way: It's an opportunity for you to answer the question: "What would you do or attempt to do if it were not possible for you to fail?"

I hope you take seriously the three elements I've asked you to bring to the dreamstorming session. In fact, I hope you will stop and deeply consider this last one before you begin. If you're like me, you take instructions like this with a grain of salt. I beg of you, please don't do that in this case. You will get out of dreamstorming what you put into it. Making the investment to be completely open-minded during your dreamstorming session will set the course for this journey.

To help you with the dreamstorming session, I'm going to provide categories to help with the thought process. Please understand that these categories are simply to provoke your thinking; they're neither concrete nor complete in their possibilities. I'm sure that we could combine some categories and possibly add others to the list. My goal here is to simply get you started. These are your dreams, and if you want to add or subtract or adapt the process in any way, I encourage you to do so.

It's important when setting out on any journey to have a goal in mind. I believe the same is true when it comes to dreamstorming. I encourage you to set a goal for how many dreams you would like to articulate.

Let's also put a few rules in place.

Number 1: There are no right or wrong dreams in a dreamstorming session.

Number 2: Don't allow yourself to be overwhelmed by concerns about whether you're putting things into the right category. The goal is to get things out of your head and heart and onto paper. We can adjust and move dreams into various categories later.

Number 3: Set aside time in your schedule to make this happen. This step alone indicates whether this is important to you or not.

Number 4: Find a place where you can conduct the dreamstorming session that is quiet or reflective or inspirational for you.

Number 5: I need you to show up! What I mean is, please don't come at this half-heartedly. Show up and give this everything that you are able.

Number 6: Start declaring the dream, baby. That's right, it's time to articulate the dream!

So, where to begin?

Let's look at some of the dreamstorming categories to help you on this Journey. Remember, these are just starting blocks to begin the process of making your list. As you begin the dreamstorming process, set a goal to come up with 8-10 dreams under each category…your goal being a list of 101 dreams!

One of the big mistakes I have seen people make as I walk them through this process is that they get too locked into the literal sense of these categories. For instance, I have people struggle with the question: "Does this fall under Physical or Material?" My perspective is that it doesn't really matter. The purpose of this exercise is to come up with a list of dreams, and the category headings are simply there to help you in putting your dreams to paper. So take a deep breath, open up your mind to "what's possible" and get ready to have fun dreaming!

Here are some Dreamstorming categories:
- Physical
- Material
- Professional
- Financial
- Adventure
- Intellectual
- Psychological
- Character
- Emotional
- Spiritual
- Creative
- Legacy

Why is articulating the dream important? As we said earlier, articulating the dream moves the dream from something that's in your head and onto paper. It takes something intangible and makes it tangible. Something powerful happens in our lives when we write things down. When you write your dreams down, you give your dreams value. I believe this is crucial because your dreams are an extension of your person; when you give value to your dreams, you are giving value to yourself.

Articulating our dreams simply means talking about them. It means that we are open with others about our dreams. It means we are open with ourselves about our dreams. Think about it: If I have something valuable and I don't share it with others, then, really, how valuable is it? Think about this as well: The more I talk about something, the more real it becomes to me.

When I articulate my dreams—meaning I write them down and talk about them—two things happen. First, I begin to move the universe in such a way as to attract elements of my dreams that will help make my dreams a reality; and secondly, I will become more aware of my surroundings and opportunities as they arise.

Let me break those two things down for you. If you are familiar with the concept of *The Secret*, articulated in a book by Rhonda Byrne, then you will understand the first reference. Essentially the belief behind "the secret" is that as I speak my truth, my reality, into the universe, I attract or create that reality in my life. While you may not fully embrace this concept, I'm sure the core principle is one you can get behind. It's like this: As I talk to others about my dreams, those individuals become aware of my dreams and in so doing can support my dreams directly or indirectly, by helping to connect me with others. If I don't talk about my dreams, then others don't know about my dreams, and I miss opportunities because of that.

I do believe that there is some value in speaking my dreams. If nothing else, you can simply call it prayer. Pray for the things you want in life. The Bible tells us to ask and we will receive. Many of us never receive because we never ask. *Asking* is articulating. Articulating is being vocal about our dreams and allowing others to participate in our dreams.

The second principle, of being *aware*, is simply that the more I talk about something, the more aware I am of that something in my life. Let me give you an illustration to solidify this a little more. Have you ever purchased a car or some other item that you were convinced very few others owned? But then, having bought it, you notice that everyone around you seems to have the same item? It's because you are more aware of your surroundings. It's not that everyone rushed out and purchased the same car you did at the same moment. As we articulate our dreams and speak openly about our dreams, we become more aware of our surroundings and the opportunities that arise to help us achieve our dreams.

For some, articulating the dream can be the scariest step in the process, because it begins to put feet to the journey of the dreamer. As you begin to articulate your dreams you find yourself brushing up against feelings or emotions that aren't pleasant or normal. I would caution you not to give up on the process at this stage because of how you experience it. You are entering new ground, beginning a new journey. Many of us are tapping into something that has lain dormant for years, and for a reason. Knocking on the door of your dreams can be a scary proposition, but it is something that will change your life if you allow it.

I encourage you to take the step of the dreamer and begin to articulate your dreams. Ask and you will receive. Seek and you will find. Articulate and let the journey begin!

Now is the time to focus on Beliefs and Behaviors:

Application Questions:
- What dreams have you not articulated often (or ever)? What is keeping you from sharing those dreams now?

- What would you do orattempt to do if it were not possible for you to fail?
- How can you take the Dreamstorming process to a new level?

Action Items:
- Spend a few hours Dreamstorming: follow the plan laid out in the book
- Invite friends and family to join you in the Dreamstorming Process
- Share your Dreamstorming List on the JOTD Facebook Page
  [visit www.thejourneyofthedreamer.com/worksheets for a Dreamstorm sheet]

Architect the Dream

When I think about architecture, I think about a plan, a framework, blueprints designed to create something magnificent. The same is true when it comes to dreaming.

The next step is to architect the dream—that is, to create a plan of action in order to achieve the dream. One thing I have found as I have worked with people on their dreams is that many of them have dreams and can talk about them, but don't have a clue as to how to make them a reality. You need a plan.

There are many ways to go about this. Depending on your make-up and personality, you might choose one of two options I will detail here. I find that those who are engineers by trade tend to want more time and thought when building out the plan. Conversely, those who are quick to act and tend to fly by the seat of their pants tend to like a plan that is quick and agile.

Before we look at these models we need to take a moment to determine which dream we plan to achieve. If you did dreamstorming correctly, you should have a list of 101 dreams. Why 101? Honestly, because I just love that number! It's greater than 100, and I am sure that most of you would tell me you couldn't come up with a list of 100. BUT with the Dreamstorming categories mentioned earlier, it should feel more realistic to come up with that many. It would be quite a feat to tackle all of them at once. I encourage people to review the list and consider which of the dreams feels most pressing or most easily achieved.

One simple way to do this is to grade your dreams: A, B, and C. A would be short-term, B mid-range and C a long-term dream. Once you've determined the time frame for each item, you can go about looking at the dreams from the perspective of what is most near and dear to your heart. The goal is to determine the dreams that have the biggest bang for the buck: those dreams we can achieve quickly and get some wins under our belt. At this point, it is as much a morale boost as anything else.

For whatever reason, whether it's the limitations of time, energy, or ability, we have not gone after our dreams. For the dream process to be successful, we need to achieve some dreams and feel the passion and exhilaration that flows from achieving them. Therefore look at your list and determine which of your short-term dreams you can achieve quickly, and which of them would mean the most to you if you could achieve them. Look at your dreams and think about which ones really speak to your heart! if there are any dreams on your list that really excite you or give you goosebumps thinking about, those would be dreams that I would consider putting at the top of your list.

Now that you have a list of dreams you would like to achieve, let's look at the action plan models we can use to help us.

The first is a three-step model that's quick, efficient and can be adapted often through your journey.

Simply put, it involves outcomes, assets and behaviors. Outcomes are the end results, that is, the desires we wish to achieve. Assets are the tools and resources we have available to us or that we need to have available to us to achieve the desired outcomes. Behaviors are simply the actions we need to take to reach those outcomes.

If you sketch this out correctly, the model can actually look like a tree, because at times the behavior is a new outcome that we need to achieve, and sometimes the behavior is that we need assets that we need to gather around us. Don't be surprised if, as you get into this model, you begin to really dive deep and create a spider web of activity.

Let's take an example of a dream from your list. Let's say your dream is to take the family to Disneyland. That's a dream for many people. So we will write out, at the top of the left column on the page, Outcome, and beneath that: "Take the family to Disneyland." To make an outcome stick or make it actionable, we need to give it a time frame, so underneath your outcome I want you to put down a time you would like to achieve this outcome, let's say, by December 2020. That would be a good start.

Next, under the second column, Assets, we need to think about the assets we need to achieve the dream, in this case to take the family to Disneyland. You can even split your asset list into two columns: assets you have and assets you'll need. Or brainstorm all of the assets you'll need and then just put a in H beside the ones you have and an N beside the ones you need. Simple.

In the assets list will be items such as a budget, vacation time, money, plane tickets, airfare, hotel, park tickets, suitable clothes, etc. You get the idea. To achieve an outcome you need resources to make it happen. That's the point of the asset list. Now, some of these play off of each other. You won't know exactly how much money you need until you have a budget set, for example. Once you have your list then you can figure out the priorities and begin to take the steps to make the dream a reality.

Finally, we create our Behaviors list. This is really the nuts and bolts of the plan. You're going to write down the actions you need to perform to achieve the desired outcome. Don't worry about the order; just make the list and then reorder it. Personally I find it's best to just get things out of my head and onto paper, and then I can organize it. Otherwise I try to do too much at once and forget steps and what was on my mind because I was preoccupied with something else. It's easier to follow the brainstorm principle: write it down and deal with organizing it later. It doesn't have to be right or wrong the first time.

On your behaviors list you'll need to include things like create a budget, which in itself prompts new behaviors. We would need to research, for example, how much tickets will cost, and the price of other assets we listed. So maybe a behavior then would be to research ticket prices. Look at your asset list and create a behaviors list from it: research cost of Disneyland tickets, research cost of plane tickets, research cost of hotel, research cost of rental car, etc. Don't take any action yet. What we're doing is creating a behavior list, an action list. Keep going! Once you've created a budget list and done the research, you'll need to take other actions: Purchase tickets. Reserve hotel. Purchase airline tickets. Ask for time off work. You get the idea.

If this sounds like a lot, another behavior you might write down would be to contact a travel agent to do much of this for you. Looking for alternatives is a reality when working towards an outcome. Sometimes we have to reframe the outcome. Let's say that, as you're writing these things down, you realize you just don't have the time to do it. Do you give up on the dream? No, you reframe the dream and figure out a workaround, like getting a travel agent to take some of the burden and allow you to achieve the dream without taking up all of your time.

The second planning model, that would be a bit more agile and fluid, is to take time to sit down with pen and paper and being making a list. Essentially you will go through the process outlined below:

- Dream Name
- What is the value in achieving this dream? Why is it important to you?
- What action steps need to happen in order for you to achieve your dream?
- I break these steps down into 3 categories:
  - A: 2-4 Hours of time
  - B: 1-2 Hours of time
  - C: Less than an Hour
  - D: Quick Wins (something that can happen quickly)
- Think of this as if we are going to "budget energy and time"…now we need to put these actions on the calendar
- Next take the various action steps and create them as calendar appointments, so as to block off your calendar and your time

I know it sounds a bit more involved but I find this model very effective! Brendon Burchard has a saying that I absolutely love, "Ambition sucks without a calendar!" By breaking your tasks down and physically adding them to your calendar, you are giving them value and making a commitment to yourself to complete the tasks that you have created for your dream…thus ensuring greater success at achieving said dream.

Now is the time to focus on Beliefs and Behaviors:

Application Questions:
- Have you take time to develop a plan to achieve your dreams?
- What dream(s) do you have on your list that you could *architect* and *achieve* quickly?
- What limitations are keeping you from truly going after your dreams?

Action Items:
- Select a model for *architecting* your dream and create a plan today:
- Use the *outcomes, actions and behaviors* model to map out a dream.
- Use the second model of planning to draft your dream plan.
  [visit www.thejourneyofthedreamer.com/worksheets for the planning sheets]

Achieve the Dream

After you've spent time articulating the dream and architecting the dream, the next is to achieve the dream. It may sound obvious, yet this is the part where most people trip up. I don't know how many people I've talked to who have a plan for what they need to do and have told other people what they are going to do, but never actually go out and do it. This is the place where most people get stalled on the way to living the dream life.

Achieving the dream can happen two different ways.

Just getting out and doing it can be done on your own. It can be something that is for you and about you and all you. But I'd love to challenge that thinking and invite you to consider the possibility of inviting others to join you as you achieve the dream.

One of the biggest challenges is to stick with the plan you have written out. You articulated the dream. You spent time telling people about the dream. You spent time describing what the dream is. You spent time working on the dream. You architected the dream. You built a plan for how the dream would happen. Now, work the plan. Go do what it is you said you would do, but along the way, invite others to come with you on the journey as you make that dream a reality. There are several ways you can do that.

First, you can assemble a team of people willing to encourage and support you on the journey, people who will hold you accountable, people who perhaps have done something similar before, who can cheer you on as you're making it happen, who will follow you on the way.

The second thing you can do is invite somebody to work on the dream with you, someone who will be part of it with you so that it becomes a reality for them as well.

This concept is something I was introduced to several years ago by an author whom I met when I worked at Zappos. Keith Ferrazzi wrote *Never Eat Alone*, and the conversation he and I had around the principle behind the book has stuck with me ever since. We do so many things, all the time, on our own. Why not do it with someone? Why not have someone you can do the journey with? There may be others out there who want to live out a particular dream just as you do, but don't have the support structure you have. Perhaps this is a friend or marriage partner who is interested in doing the dream just like you. So why not invite that person to be part of the journey?

The amazing thing about this now, in our society and culture, is that it you can accomplish your dreams in partnership with someone who isn't even in the same vicinity. In some cases, you might do it virtually, with someone on the other side of the world, or with someone on Facebook. You could do a Facebook Live or streaming event together. You could gather multiple people at the same time in different areas of the world and do it all at the same day at the same time and post pictures together. Think outside the box when you're talking about achieving the dream. Don't get locked into the idea that you have to have somebody right beside you physically on your way to make this happen. Build a community of people; build your team. Invite people to join you. Never dream alone. Go after it and make it happen.

Another thing you could do along the way is to get a coach. You could hire one or just ask someone to offer their time to help you stay focused on the dream, making sure that everything you have articulated and architected is something you're actually going to do. Coaching could be informal, delivered by a friend or someone you know that can give you support, can walk with you along the way, hold you accountable to the things that you need to say and the things that you need to do. Or it could be a more formal relationship, someone you reach out to or hire to help you along the journey. However you choose to do it, get a coach—especially when you are going for a dream that is outside your comfort zone.

While we're talking about that, let's look at the dream list you've created. You've architected this dream list and now a plan for how to accomplish it. Remember, you've got a list. Keep that list growing; keep adding to it regularly. I encourage people to shoot for a list of at least 101 dreams right away, but build that list on a regular basis. It should be dynamic, not static. Make it something that you're continually thinking about and working on, working through, and drawing up plans to achieve.

Remember to begin with the kind of dreams that are low-hanging fruit—a bit easier to work on and quicker to achieve—but will have decent impact on your life. Go for those first. It's all about building momentum and a sense of energy as you stack up successes.

As you build on those successes, you'll find you get better at achieving your dreams, and you'll start to take more risks when it comes to getting there. Some of the dreams you've written down and articulated, which may seem to be way out there and could never happen, suddenly come to the forefront. Some dreams you'd been thinking about for years, about which you had no idea how to make them happen, now seem a bit more doable, thanks to your support system: your team, your coach, and so forth. I urge you to go after those dreams with everything you've got.

My encouragement is to set a goal for how many dreams you're going to achieve, on a regular basis. Every year I come up with a list of 52 in 52, meaning: 52 dreams that I want to achieve in 52 weeks. My goal at the beginning of the year is to focus on one dream a week. It doesn't always work out that way, of course, but setting that as an intention gets me moving in right direction. By the end of the year I want to achieve that list of 52. Now, what's funny is, even though I've done this many times, I still find that my list changes and adjusts during the year. Just this year I put down that I wanted to go to a Tony Robbins event. I have wanted to for years and have never gotten around to it. While I was looking at various dates and locations for upcoming Tony Robbins' events, I had the privilege of attending a Brendon Burchard event. When I took a step back to think about what I wanted from the Robbins event (strategies and frameworks for becoming my best self, delivered by one of the leading voices in the positive psychology field) I realized that I got that (and more) from Burchard's High Performance Academy. I reframed the dream (instead of going to a Tony Robbins event, I got what I was looking for from Brendon's event) and checked it off my list because I had achieved what I truly had set out to do.

Another dream I had was to design a tattoo. But instead of actually creating the design, I brought some elements together, took them to a tattoo artist whom I trust and whose work I respect, and allowed him to design the tattoo for me. He came up with something that's a work of art. Again: reframe the dream. I'm not an artist, but I had an idea of what I wanted. So why not take my ideas to an expert and let him help me put those ideas into something concrete?

To me, that's what it's all about. Come up with your list: What is it you're going to do? What is it you're going to achieve? What are you going to go after? Some of the dreams on my list are really simple: I want to host a dinner party. Guess what? As I write, it's May, and I think since the beginning of the year we've probably hosted three or four dinner parties already this year.

So that's what it's about. I get excited about some things that are on my list. Others, not so much. Some are bigger dreams, or dreams that I yearn for even though I don't really know exactly what they mean. One item on my list is: *Do something that's completely outside of your comfort zone.* The interesting thing about that dream for me is that, as I write it, I have in mind some things I might want to do, but when the time comes to actually make those dreams happen, my comfort zone has expanded. So some things I once thought were outside of my comfort zone are right in the middle of my comfort zone now. Again, reframe the dream.

Always remember, the journey of the dreamer is about living life to the fullest. That's the reason for articulating, sharing, writing down your dreams, creating a plan for how you'll make them happen, and taking action to make them happen.

You're on a journey of becoming your greatest self, your best self, and to make that happen you have to take steps each and every day that are outside of your comfort zone. Once you've experienced life outside of the comfort zone, the journey takes on fresh meaning. That's when you experience life to the fullest and learn more and more who you need to become. Every step along the journey, you and discover more about who you are. That's the journey of the dreamer.

Now is the time to focus on Beliefs and Behaviors:

Application Questions:
- What dream has "stalled out" for you? Why did it stall? How can you get your dream moving forward again?
- Who can you invite to join you on the Journey to help you *achieve* your dream?
- What will it feel like to *achieve* this dream?

Action Items:
- Take the plan you worked in the *Architect* section and consider the following:
  - *Articulate It*: Share it with friends and family and on Social Media
    [Make it known to the world and the people you meet]
  - *Architect It*: Plan the work and Work the plan!
- Create a Dream Team: a support team, dream partner and dream coach

Acknowledge

The next step along the journey is to acknowledge the dream. Once we acknowledge the dream, there's an awakening within us. There's a stirring in our souls, and that's where the new life begins. Once the awakening happens, awareness arises. The next three sections of this book will look in more detail at these three things: *acknowledgement, awakening* and *awareness*.

Let's jump into *acknowledgement*. Up to this point, we've just been beginning this journey. We've left the Ordinary Life and taken the journey into the Inner World, the place where a dream takes hold of us. We articulate the dream (speak it out); architect it (create a plan); then we have to achieve it.

Those three things happen again, and again, and again. It's a cycle of making these things a reality. And each time we go through that cycle, we gain strength, understanding and wisdom. Then we cycle through it again. It's almost a flywheel effect: every time we go through the cycle we gain more momentum.

Once you know you can make your dreams a reality, you'll know what you're capable of and what the process is like. You may get to the point on the flywheel where everything stops and you feel weightless—like one of those drop rides at an amusement park where you're going up, and up, and with every click upward it slows. Then you're anticipating that moment when it stops—and drops. That happens as we go through this Inner World on the way to becoming the best version of ourselves.

We articulate, architect, achieve. Each time we do it faster, with more power, strength, understanding, and wisdom. Each time we tackle a dream that's a little bit more difficult than the last, then a little bit more difficult.

Then something happens.

You're in a moment of time. You stop and recognize that there's something beyond what you're doing, and acknowledge that you have dreams that are greater. You have dreams that are deeper, more meaningful than anything you've ever done before. You have dreams that you have put in a box on the shelf and hidden away.

There's a moment when you really, truly acknowledge deep in your heart that everything you've done up to this point has been *safe*. Every dream you've achieved up to this point has been comfortable, fun, exciting. It's been valuable, even meaningful, but there's more. To move to the next level, to take dreaming to the next phase of the journey, there's a point where you have to stop thinking about dreams the way you used to. You have to stop thinking about yourself the way you used to think of yourself. This is the point in the hero's journey where the hero dies. This is the point where a sacrifice has to be made.

This is the point in the hero's journey when you are in the Abyss, and you're looking at life and everything around you and truly acknowledging that there's something deeper, that up to this point you've been playing games. Up to this point it's been fun, exciting, and energetic, but you know there's more. There's a deeper calling on your life. There are more meaningful dreams to be had, dreams greater than anything you've ever shared with anyone, dreams that you have thought of in the deep recesses of your heart that stir you with emotion, dreams that are calling out to you to truly step into your greatest self and live from the place of greatness you were created for.

Many people stand on the edge of the Abyss and retreat. They get to the very edge of glory and decide it's too much; it's too risky. They turn away. Many people will leave their gift to the world at the altar of fear and doubt because they're not willing to die to their old way of thinking: their old way of thinking about themselves that they can't achieve more, their old way of thinking that says, "You're not valuable. You're not smart enough. You don't have the resources. This is crazy. These are pipe dreams. Nobody has ever done anything like this. What have you done up to this point to think that you can do anything like this?"

The tragedy is that these fearful and doubting thoughts, more often than not, are just stories we have told ourselves, based on something others have said. They're not even based in reality. Because of somebody else's fear, or doubt, or insecurity, they made a comment that we have claimed as our own truth. In the moment when we're faced with our greatness, in the moment we acknowledge that there's more to life than what we've been living, at the moment we acknowledge that our greatest self is calling us, we allow the voices of the past, the voices of others, the pain of the past, our doubts, insecurities, and fears to step in and keep us from taking the single greatest step in the journey of the dreamer.

I beg you, if you're in this moment, and there's something stirring deep within you, maybe even haunting your visions at night, something that gives you sparks of wonder or goosebumps, don't turn away in fear. Acknowledge that those dreams, those opportunities for greatness, are there. Acknowledge that they exist.

This is taking the articulating part of the journey to a deeper level. This means articulating dreams you have never talked about before. This becomes an opportunity to take something great to a deeper level, to share your greatness with people you've never shared your dreams with before. I believe the reason this is so scary for many people is because such dreams are truly connected to your soul, your deepest self. The fear is this: When I put these dreams out there, how will people respond? What will people do? What if they don't like it? What if I'm not accepted? What if it's not good enough? What if I fail?

While all those questions are legitimate, what if the exact opposite of what we fear comes to pass? You see, we get caught up in the negative narrative. What if, when we put ourselves out there, we're *not* rejected by the masses, but accepted? What if, instead of people shying away from us and walking away, they are attracted to us? What if, instead of people not appreciating what we have to say, what we have to say changes their lives? What if, instead of mocking us, people praise us and thank us? What if, instead of making people laugh, our dreams cause people to love?

I understand, it's risky. I've been there. This book is that dream for me. This book has been almost five years in the making, and several times almost didn't come to fruition, or to print. Even as I write these words I have no idea what's going to happen with this book, but I know that this is a dream and a defining moment for me. I will no longer allow my fears and doubts to control my dreams and my destiny. I am no longer going to offer up my dreams, my gifts, my abilities, my talents at the altar of fear and doubt. In this moment, I am acknowledging a deeper dream. I am acknowledging that this book is the first step in a deeper dream, and that it opens the doors for me to be able to change the lives of thousands of people, because I believe that this is a life-changing message.

I believe that there are thousands and thousands of people who let the stories that others have shared and the stories others have created keep them from living the life they desire and deserve. My dream is to be the champion of those individuals, the one who calls them out of the Ordinary Life to take the risk, to step into the Inner World and see what they're made of, to experience what life is like when they achieve their dreams, and then to come to that moment when they are challenged to step outside of their comfort zone, to step to the edge of their greatest self, put everything on the line and acknowledge that they have so much more to offer. That's the step of acknowledgement. That's what I want for each of you.

As you read these words, my prayer is that when a little glimpse of greatness pops up for you, instead of quickly brushing it away, or denying or devaluing it, you will take a moment and write it down. Take articulation to a whole new level and begin to acknowledge the deeper dreams living within you. Let's let the old way of thinking die, so that we can enter into a new life, a new way of thinking, a new way of achieving the dream, and living the dream life, and becoming your greatest self.

Now is the time to focus on Beliefs and Behaviors:

Application Questions:
- You have been on the Journey for a while, what do you need to acknowledge about your process thus far? Strengths? Struggles? Successes? Stand stills?
- What is the "deeper call" taking place in your life?
- What dream is calling to you from a deep place that you've been avoiding?

Action Items:
- Take a moment to stop and consider all that is happening on this Journey:
  - Who are you becoming?
  - What has happened for you so far?
  - How are you feeling about the Journey? About your progress?
- Spend time this week writing in a journal about the dream process. Recognize all that has been taking place within and without.
- Share your newly acknowledged dream with your Dream Team and on the Journey of the Dreamer Facebook Page.

Awareness

After you've acknowledged the dream, and the deepest part of it, the next step along the journey is awareness. Acknowledgment brings awareness of several things.

First, you become more aware of who you really are and who you were meant to be. And this awareness is huge. It happens on the journey partly because you've already done the first part. You've already articulated, architected, and achieved several dreams, and you had the opportunity to see exactly what you're made of.

With this awareness of who you are, you become more aware of your calling in life, your purpose, your mission. Write those things down. In the realm of personal development, purpose statements—or mission statements—are highly regarded as the first step in the journey. I don't know if it's the first step, but it certainly is a step to begin to articulate your mission statement, to think concretely about your purpose in life.

It's not just about what you're going to do. It's about who you are, who you need to become along the way. That's what I mean about becoming the hero of your journey, the hero of your own life and of the lives you will have an impact on along the way. As you step outside your comfort zone and realize who you really are, you'll become aware of your strengths and weaknesses and of areas in your life where you have an opportunity to grow.

You can spend time working on those areas of your life, developing your skills to make them a reality. If there are areas where you feel you need to grow, develop, or simply understand better, and that you'll be held back in achieving your dreams until you do, this may be an opportunity, again, to invite someone else to help you along the journey.

One of my dreams is to, within 10 years, own my own pub. I love the idea of having a place where we can have soccer on the telly, where people can gather and enjoy each other's company, where we can showcase local food and drink, have local bands play. I look forward to owning a place where people can be themselves and enjoy an atmosphere of joy, energy, and excitement.

But the reality is, I've never done anything like that. I don't know the first thing about running a pub. So to make this dream a reality, I'm going to need help. I will need a manager, investors, and input from people who have done this before. And I know that. It doesn't make the dream any less valuable, important or desirable. It just means I have to ask for help.

Knowing that now, I am more aware when I'm having conversations with people about who they are, what gifts they might bring. In conversations, I become aware of my strengths, and of my opportunities to grow in this dream. I become aware of what others might be able to bring to the table. I'm becoming more aware of other people who may have a similar dream.

Part of the process of making something like this happen is simply talking about our deeper dreams. Remember, we've acknowledged them, but we also need to begin the process of articulating those dreams, sharing them with others. Because these are the deep dreams of our hearts, perhaps we share them only with a tight-knit group, a select few people whom we love and trust. Then, as we gain support, we start to build that out and share it with more people. As we do this, we want to become aware of how other people may be able to enter our dreams with us, to work alongside us to make our dreams a reality.

In this process, I'm becoming more aware of my strengths and opportunities, of others who may be able to enter in, and the needs that others may have for my dreams. Now I'm listening for hints, looking for cues, paying attention to what people are saying about my dreams. That's where awareness comes in.

I've compared this process to what happens when you buy a particular model of car. I want a unique car no one else owns. I do my research: I go to car dealerships, look online, and I find my car. The day finally comes to buy it, and I'm excited. I go to the dealership, go through all the paperwork, and finally I'm sitting in my new car. I'm smelling my new car, feeling my new car, experiencing my new car at a deep, deep level, because nobody has this car.

I start the ignition, pull out of the parking lot. And on my way home—I pass my car at least eight times! Somebody else purchased my car at the same moment I bought mine, right? That's what it seems like. But the reality is, I just wasn't aware of this car passing by me every day. I wasn't aware of it until it became a conscious reality.

That's what happens in the dream process. Once I acknowledge the deep dreams of my heart, those dreams become part of me. By admitting they're there, and expressing that, I instantly become more aware of what's going on around me. I become more aware of opportunities, and of people who may play a part in accomplishing my dreams. I become more aware of my strengths and my opportunities to grow. I become more aware of exactly how important that dream is.

That, my friends, is an amazing place to come to. When I get to that place, all of a sudden I realize just how important that dream really is, and that's an amazing place to be. That's what awareness does along the journey of the dreamer. When acknowledgement and awareness meet, that leads us to the third element of this Inner World—the part where we have to die to our old way of thinking and stop allowing voices from the past to lead us into fear, doubt, and insecurity. That leads us to the point where we realize our greatness, our genius, our unique gift, our unique voice, and our opportunity to make a difference in the world. That leads us to our awakening.

Now is the time to focus on Beliefs and Behaviors:

Application Questions:
- How has your *awareness* changed in regard to your life, purpose and mission?
- How has the Journey of the Dreamer impacted who you are, not just what you do?
- Who will you need to become more of as you move into the best version of yourself?

Action Items:
- Keep an active journal throughout your day and make a list of interactions, events, circumstances, etc. that have to do with your dreams.
- Share your dreams with 3 new people this week!
- Look back over your dream list and spend time considering how these dreams are showing up in your life.
  [visit www.thejourneyofthedreamer.com/worksheets for a journal tracker]

Awakening

Picture a moment when all is still and quiet, all the chaos of life has stopped, the noise of life has ceased, the distractions of the mind are stilled. Imagine breathing in that stillness and exhaling the fear and the doubt. Breathe in strength and exhale insecurities. Breathe in confidence and exhale inactivity. As you take in one last deep breath, one that fills up your lungs, imagine experiencing all that life has to offer in that one moment. As you open your eyes, exhale again, and imagine awakening as you now experience your greatest self.

In that moment of awakening, when you truly realize who you were meant to be, you realize that your greatest self is not out there in the future as something to become, but who you are right now. In that moment you realize that you are the dreamer, the hero of your journey. You are the one called to make this dream a reality, and only you can do so, because of your gifts, your talents, your abilities.

You may need others along the way. In every epic tale, the hero has companions who help him or her on this path. Several of my favorite tales reflecting the hero's journey are *Star Wars, Lord of the Rings,* and *The Hobbit*. But one that I feel expresses this awakening in the most complete way is *The Matrix*. Think of the journey Neo went through, when he suddenly exited the world that for many years he had believed to be his world. He had to do exactly what we talked about at the beginning: to articulate the dream—to recognize that the Matrix was there, to recognize that he was looking for Morpheus. Then he had to architect the dream—to figure out a way to get out of The Matrix—by creating a plan with the help of Morpheus. Then he had to achieve the dream—he had to take the pill.

In that moment, he stepped into reality. In that moment, he stepped into the Inner World. In that moment, he stepped into a space where he had to acknowledge a new reality. With that acknowledgment came an awareness that maybe he was the one—or maybe not—but regardless, he had to start taking steps to save his friends, to be greater than he had been up to that point.

The awakening moment for me comes at the end of the movie, when the agents are there and they think they've defeated him, and he wakes up, breathes in that breath, opens his eyes, and looks around. Instead of seeing the visuals, the colors, the imprints on the mind that he had been seeing up to that point, now he sees everything in code. He sees the Matrix for what it really is. In that moment, he realizes that he is *the one*.

That's what we're talking about here. There will come a point along the journey when everything seems to end, everything seems to stop. A point when you feel like you've done everything you can do to push the dream along. You've stepped into your greatest self as much as you know how. You've done the things you needed to do to make the dream a reality. You've asked people to help along the way. You're aware of your surroundings. You've acknowledged that there's something deeper.

Then there's a point when the dream seems to die. When you feel like you have no more strength to give, like there's nothing left in the tank. When you doubt yourself, you doubt your worth, you doubt your ability to make this happen. You may come to a point when you even doubt if the dream is real—or even worth it.

In that moment, when you feel all hope is lost, when the dream has died, or worse, the dreamer has died, you'll close your eyes. And then you'll breathe in again, and experience a bit of life, and exhale. And you breathe in again, and now there's a little more strength, and then you exhale. And you breathe in and the dream now becomes more vibrant, and you exhale. When you take this next breath in, it's almost as if you don't have the dream anymore, but now the dream has you and has given you a new life, a new passion, a new purpose, a new presence, a new strength, a new energy to tackle the journey.

Instead of dying, the dream has created in you the strength and ability to get up, to open your eyes, to wake up to new surroundings and a new way of viewing things, to a new way of seeing yourself. All of a sudden, you are the hero of your own journey. You don't *think* you are. You *know* you are. You don't see your greatest self *out there*. You *are* your greatest self. You don't see the dream as something to be achieved, but rather something that's alive in you. The dream is something that's motivating you, causing you to live in a new state and to function at a higher frequency.

The dream is now awakening in you a desire to make it happen at all costs. In that moment, it's not a question of "Can I do this?"—it's a reality that you *will* do this, that this dream is going to happen. In fact, that it has already happened, and you need to take just a few more steps to bring it to completion.

That's the awakening. That's the moment that the journey of the dreamer becomes the journey of the doer. That's the moment that the deeper dreams in the recesses of your heart aren't just lofty goals that you hope to achieve some day, but what drives your every breath, your every step, your every moment, your every thought. That's the moment when the dream becomes real and the dreamer becomes the doer, the hero of your own journey, the hero of your life, the hero of your dreams. It's all part of the journey.

In that moment, you can't rely on the stories of the past, of your mistakes, as representing reality. Everything that's happened in the past happened for you to get you to this point, so that you could experience a new life, an awakened life. A life where there is no box. Or, to keep *The Matrix* imagery going, a life where there is no spoon. A reality that you design, a reality that you create, a reality that you enact because you are the hero. You are the one in your dream. You are the one in your reality.

Now you have a new sense, a new passion, a new desire to take this dream back to others, to take this dream to the world, to give this gift to the world, because you know in your heart and with every fiber of your being that this is what you were called to. This is what you were created for. This is your masterpiece, and your calling in life is now to go and take this to the world.

Allow that awakening to happen within you. Allow the dream to have you. In that moment, experience what it is to be your greatest self. That's the awakening. That's the power of the journey of the dreamer.

As you begin to take that back, as you begin to live in a new strength, a new reality, a new vibrance, as you begin to operate at a new frequency, you will take that back. Instead of entering the Ordinary Life that you left, you will now enter the Extraordinary Life, a world that is brand-new, a world that you create and design. Allow the awakening to happen within the deepest recesses of your soul and have the courage to be made new. Have the courage to allow the dream to have you.

Now is the time to focus on Beliefs and Behaviors:

Application Questions:
- What "movie moments" give you goosebumps and stir deep within you? What are these moments saying to your heart? What are they telling you about you?
- Who would you become in that moment you leave behind your fear and doubt and fully embrace your greatness?
- What dream would you go after once you have fully awakened to your strength?

Action Items:
- Consider meditating and practice being "in the moment" 3 times this week.
  - Take in strength and confidence
  - Release fear and doubt
- Make a list of all of the movies that stir you deeply and identify what these moments are call you to.
- Say Goodbye: Once you have come to grips with the *awakening* and what you need to let go of, hold a ceremony and say goodbye to that which is holding you back!

5 Essentials of the Extraordinary Life

Now that we have gone through the Inner World, we're going to come back out into the outer world. Instead of going back to the Ordinary Life, we're going to enter the Extraordinary Life. What has to happen for you to live the Extraordinary Life?

There are five essentials to living the Extraordinary Life.

The first essential is *pleasure*. We're going to do things that bring us pleasure, things that we like, things we enjoy. We'll talk about that a little bit more in-depth.

Next is *passion*. Passion is the next level or layer, which goes deeper. The things we're passionate about are things that speak to the deeper parts of who we are and what we're about.

From there we move on to *purpose*, which goes to the deepest part of who we are, to explore our sense of mission and calling.

Then the next essential is *practice*. We'll start to add important practices into our lives and daily routines. To become experts in these areas, really dig in, and make them part of our life, not just things we do every once in a while.

Then finally, we step into the last essential, an essential of *peace*. Ultimately, that's what we're after. The journey of the dreamer is about getting to a place of peace, fulfillment, and contentment. We're not talking about a peace that happens because of an emptiness or a void. We're talking about a peace that comes from the activity that we've been involved in. A peace that comes from the fulfillment and satisfaction of knowing that we did everything we could do.

We'll look more closely at these five essentials of living the Extraordinary Life in the following chapters: pleasure, passion, purpose, practice and peace.

Pleasure

To live a life of pleasure means we get to do the things that we want to do. Remember, we've just come back from the Inner World, the space of Testing and Trials and the Journey Hom. We've come back from a place where life has changed, where the things that we once knew, clung to and enjoyed may have changed.

We want to experience new pleasures in life, but it starts with things that are familiar. You can make a list of the things you simply enjoy doing: Maybe it's picnics, going for walks, playing video games, watching movies, or listening to music. What are the activities you just truly enjoy? This is important to note, because having them on this list means you've already got some wins under your belt. Again, we're coming back to a new life, a new normal: the

Extraordinary Life. We want to do things that are comfortable, but it's important to recognize where we have changed.

As you come back to some of the things you used to find enjoyable, you may find them less enjoyable now. Some things that maybe once scared you are now the very things that excite you and energize you. My suggestion is to make a list of the things that you once did that were exciting, that brought you energy, that were fun. Now go through them one by one.

This is the foundation of my "52 in 52" list every year. I typically begin by listing the things I just enjoy doing. I enjoy volunteering at soup kitchens and serving other people. I enjoy getting tattoos. I enjoy going to baseball games. I enjoy going for hikes. Make a list of your own. As you ponder that list, you may find that there are some elements of it you just don't enjoy anymore, and that's okay. You can choose not to do those things anymore. You may also discover there are things on the list you do enjoy doing that you didn't used to do. Don't be afraid to add to this list in an ongoing way. It should be something that's dynamic, something you're adding to on a regular basis. Try out new things. Remember, this is the new you, this is a new life. Part of the new life is to try new things. My encouragement to you is to try something new once a month. If listening to live music wasn't on your list until now, maybe go to a concert. If you didn't in the past enjoy a certain type of food, give it a try and see what happens, see what kind of space opens up for you as you expand your tastes.

This space of pleasure is so important, because it fulfills some of our evolved desires. Sometimes I just want to eat a cheeseburger. And guess what? In moderation, that's okay. Sometimes I just want to get crazy and dance. When I'm alone, that's okay. If you find enjoyment and pleasure in something and it's not harming anyone, it's not illegal or immoral, then I say: Go for it! That's a big step toward living the dream life, and putting into practice everything you've learned so far.

Passion

The next level is passion. This refers to things that aren't just enjoyable or exciting, but where I find life. I'm passionate about my heritage. I'm passionate about serving others. Those aren't just things I enjoy, they're things I'm passionate about, that I'm driven towards.

One way to express the difference is what happens if I want to see a particular movie but miss it at the local theater. If it's just a matter of pleasure, that's okay; I'll catch it when it comes out on DVD. But if it's on a theme I'm really passionate about, my attitude is quite different. I connect with some of the Marvel characters and feel like I've done life with them, so for me going to those movies is a passion, and I'll drop everything to be there on opening night.

Similarly, my Scottish heritage is a passion for me, something with which I'm deeply connected. I don't just enjoy going to the Scottish games, I want to be part of the Scottish games. I want to be part of the narrative that is my ancestry, because I'm passionate about it.

When you find something you're passionate about, there's a deep element of life involved; not just excitement, but an energy that goes much deeper, that speaks to something within you and helps you draw out some of your best self.

This is deeper than pleasure, because it gives you life. In a way, it invests in you. It's not just doing something because it feels good, but rather because you get a deeper benefit from it. It adds value to who you are and what you're about. Sometimes, a passion begins with doing something pleasurable, until you find deeper reasons for doing it because of the value it brings to your life. Then it becomes a passion.

Take sports, for example. Perhaps there's a certain team you like to follow, and if that team isn't playing you won't bother going to the game. But if you're passionate about the game itself, you'll enjoy watching the game regardless of who's playing. That's passion. Pleasure may be that you enjoy watching a game on television. Passion is when you go and you follow the team around to away games. Pleasure may be something you do from time to time. Passion is something you make sure is added to your schedule and calendar on a regular basis. Passion delivers something within you. Making it happen adds value to your life.

So, one of the steps to living the Extraordinary Life is to live a life of passion. Get passionate in life, and bring that passion into every area of your life.

Purpose

All right, so far we've talked about experiencing the Extraordinary Life. Next, we'll look at what it means to live a life of purpose. You'll notice that these essentials build on each other. You do things you enjoy: that's living a life of pleasure. You do things that bring value to your life: that's living a life of passion. To live a life of purpose, you look for things that bring meaning or ultimate value to your life. This means living in the space that drives you, that moves you forward, that puts you in another realm, as it were.

I used to be of the mindset that when you based your life on purpose, that you had to have one purpose, one mission, one calling, one thing in life to do, and you had to figure out what that was. I remember being in Bible college, hearing about "God's purpose for your life" and thinking: *Man, I've got to find that one thing, that needle in the haystack that God has called me to do*. I don't believe that's the case anymore. I believe that you have a calling, a mission, a purpose in life, and I believe that that purpose will shift and adjust and evolve as you grow, throughout your life.

It's possible to spend so much time trying to discover that one perfect purpose statement that you become paralyzed in a state of inaction. The way to begin to understand your purpose is to start with pleasure—find things that you enjoy doing—and notice the things that begin to add value to your life, that give you fresh energy—places of passion.

From there, you may find something that begins to feel like a calling; something you just have to do. And that's where purpose steps into the picture. As you lean into those areas of purpose, and mission, and calling, and start to work out what that means for you, you'll find another space of mission, and purpose, and calling, and then another. It builds and evolves as you grow.

The diagram next to this illustrates how to find your purpose. I hope you find it helpful. If you're trying to figure out your purpose, I believe there are three areas to look at that will help you.

One is experiences: Make a list of all the experiences—work, personal life, financial, spiritual, whatever—that have brought you to the place where you are now.

The second is education: Obviously, this is important, even though many people are paying for a good education that they end up not using directly in their careers. There are things you've learned that will help you, whether it's at the level of high school, college, master's degree, post-graduate work. Did you go to the School of Hard Knocks? Do you have certificates and certifications? What degrees did you go after?

Thirdly: enjoyment. What are the things I enjoy? Who are the people I like to be with? Where do I like to go? What do I like to do? What are the things I like to have?

As you write all this down, you can begin to home in on what makes you who you are, and that brings some kind of clarity. If you're trying to figure out what your purpose is, begin with making these lists.

Look at your experiences, education, and enjoyment, and consider whether there's any overlap. Delve into the spaces where there is overlap. Play with the possibilities: is there an area of purpose for you in those spaces?

Here is an example of what I mean:

- Experiences:
  - Teaching small groups of people
  - Training larger groups of people
  - Coaching and counseling individuals
- Education:
  - Getting a degree in training, developing speeches, etc.
  - Attending seminars on public speaking
- Enjoyment:
  - Speaking in front of various groups
  - Teaching or training others

With the example above, the purpose may be along the lines of trainer, public speaker, author or coach. I know this may seem obvious, but that may be true of your purpose as well. The reality is that most of us underestimate our strengths because they are our strengths, and most of us underestimate our purpose because it is so near and dear to us that we feel it can't be that simple.

If this example gives you some ideas, then try writing out your own list. What are your experiences? What is your education? What do you truly enjoy doing? Make your list, summarize the results and begin to live it out. Maybe you'll learn that what you once thought was your purpose isn't anymore. Maybe something that wasn't your purpose now is. Remember, you've just come through a new phase in your journey that's brought you where you are now. A lot has changed, and you've adapted. So it's okay if your sense of purpose evolves, too.

Listen, I'm of the mindset that as you're going after your dream, your pleasures, your passions and your purpose will evolve. That assumption that everything will change needs to be baked into everything you do on this journey. As you grow and live a life of purpose, your purpose will evolve with it. So be prepared for that.

Never settle for mediocrity. Never settle for going through the motions. Never settle for one-and-done. Stay in a state of perpetual motion, and activity, and action. And as your sphere of experience and education and enjoyment expands, your sphere of purpose will grow and mature. That is what living the dream life is all about. And then we move into the next phase, the one most people struggle with: Practice.

Practice

Now that we've gone through creating habits in our lives that will move us in the direction of our dreams, we've got to make sure we're continually working on them and integrating them into our lives. Practice is key, because this is where we gain mastery and gain the excitement, energy and satisfaction of knowing that we're working towards something great.

I know what it's like to try something and then back away from it because I didn't succeed. I've been there, done that, got the T-shirt, and I don't really want to go back there again. I want to become an expert. I want to become knowledgeable in something. I want to be able to pass on that knowledge to others, to experience something time and again, and do it in a way that I can really dig into it and understand it. And that's where practice comes into play.

You start to introduce things in your life that you are passionate about. Why? Because passion is at the heart of everything; it invades our minds and hearts, and gives us life. We start doing things in which we find purpose and meaning. Why? Again, because it gives us life, and as we practice the skills over and over, the more times we do it, the more life we get, the better we understand it, the more we enjoy it. Well-practiced habits become part of us. We no longer have to think about it; we're able to just make it happen.

You've heard the statement that practice makes perfect, and that's not really what I'm trying to communicate. I don't believe that practice makes perfect. I believe perfect practice makes perfect. You've got to practice something perfectly over and over to make it perfect. But if we want to make something a routine, a habit, an ingrained part of our lives, we have to practice.

One thing that makes this practice amazing is when we invite others to join us. You do something once, you might have somebody come with you. You do something twice, you're more than likely to have somebody come with you. You do something multiple times, do it over and over again, and every time you do it, invite somebody new to join with you. Now you're passing on that passion, that pleasure, and perhaps that purpose, as you invite others to join you on the journey. That to me is where it's at.

Remember, you've just walked through this valley. You're learning new skills as you go, trying out new things, succeeding at some, not succeeding at others—and it's all okay. Practice, practice, practice: that's how all the greats have become great. All of the thought leaders, the guides, the superstars that we look to for inspiration, motivation, challenge and direction—they've all practiced over and over and over again.

In *Outliers*, Malcolm Gladwell makes the point that people don't become experts because they were born at the right time or because they were genetically disposed to it. They become experts in their field or craft because they took advantage of the opportunities that were out there—and they practiced their skill at least ten thousand hours.

If you want to know what you could possibly be an expert at, think about what you've spent ten thousand hours on. Look at your life, your past experiences and where you are now, and if you can notice anywhere where you've spent ten thousand hours of activity, put in ten thousand hours of "sweat equity," that may be an area of expertise for you. That may be your genius. That may be the field where you will excel and become the next thought leader or the next superhero.

I want you to stop and really consider this area of practice and how important it is. You're on a journey towards becoming the best version of yourself. As you have figured out by now, the journey of the dreamer isn't just about dreaming; it's about doing. You can't just sit back and look at areas of your life where you find enjoyment and think wishfully, *Oh, it would be great to do that because I get a bit excited about it and it starts to give me life.* You have to say to yourself: *I'm going to do this because that is what dreamers do.*

Dreamers do the *do*. They don't just lie around and dream. Dreamers do the *do*. They spend time working on their dreams and really going after them. And they do it through the art of practice. So what are you practicing?

Peace

The last stage we're going to talk about is *peace*. I bring this up because I think this is ultimately what dreaming is about. Most of us have this idea, this splinter of a thought about what we want to go after, a dream that's part of who we are that we're striving to make a reality. But ultimately, what we want from the dream life, when we think about, as Matthew Kelly calls it, our richly imagined future, we imagine ourselves in a state of peace.

Oh, if I could have this, if I could accomplish this, if I could do this, if I could become this, then I'd be in a place of peace. When that happens, I'll experience true contentment and satisfaction and joy—peace. That's ultimately what we're going after in the journey of the dreamer. The reality is, you don't have to wait. You can have it along the way. You can experience peace while you're going after your dreams, as you articulate and architect and achieve your dreams. You can have the end result along the journey. Peace is a state of mind.

Peace happens because you are *doing the do* and becoming the person you need to become to make your dreams a reality. Peace happens because, with every step you take through pleasure and passion and purpose and practice, you become a better version of yourself. Every time you look fear in the eyes and say, "No more," and take a step of courage, you become a better version of yourself. You experience peace. Every time you take a risk, you become a better version of yourself and experience peace. Every time you put yourself out there and make your dreams a priority, you experience peace. Every time you give of yourself, are generous and supportive to others, every time you invite others along the journey, you experience peace. Peace is the end result. Living the dream life, I believe, is living a life of peace, and we can have that as we're going along the journey.

How can you not experience peace when you are working from a place of your truest self and deepest satisfaction, knowing that you're becoming the person you were designed and created to be? That's not to say there won't be many ups and downs, struggles and turmoil at points in the journey. It won't be easy, but as you become your greatest self, you learn to deal with the disappointments, pain and dissatisfactions of life.

My friends, what I am saying in all of this is that when you decide to take the journey of the dreamer, when you decide to start living your best life, when you decide to take action, you can experience a life of peace because you know that you have lived well, done well, and served others by becoming your greatest self. That is what the journey of the dreamer is all about. You won't be frantic, crazy, stressed out. You're not going to be agitated or irritated or fumbling, because you'll be living a life of pleasure, a life of passion, a life of purpose, a life of practice. You will experience a life of peace.

As you experience a life of peace, you'll draw others to yourself. Your life will be an example of what the dream life is all about. You'll be able to pour into others as they come and ask you about your life and your journey. Think about it: How amazing would it be if, as you began to share your own journey with them, you became the sage, the one that called them to their adventure, out of their Ordinary Life and into the Inner World, so they could experience the journey themselves? And one day, they might step out into the Extraordinary Life, calling others to an amazing adventure.

Now is the time to focus on Beliefs and Behaviors:

Application Questions:
- Are you experiencing the 5 Essentials as you move through the Journey of the Dreamer?
- What can you start doing more of in the realm of these Essentials?
- Are you comfortable with the ordinary life? How can these Essentials move you into your Extraordinary Life?

Action Items:

- Interact with the Essentials of the Extraordinary Life:
  - Pleasure
  - Passion
  - Purpose
  - Practice
  - Peace
- Consider the following questions:
  - Am I doing things that bring about _____?
  - How could I improve the space of _____ in my life?
  - What can I do this week to bring about more _____ in my life?

Begin Your Origin Story

I am into comic books. Perhaps you've picked that up through the book so far. If you knew me personally, you'd know that I'm really into comic books—not as much as some, but definitely more than others. If I had more time to devote to comics, I would, but at this point in life, I'm giving it only as much time, effort, and energy as I am able.

Here's what I love about comics and comic books: I love the origin story. Yes, the stories of the ongoing struggles and routines and the battles and the conflicts—all of those are amazing to me. I love how comic book writers have been able to use an art form to create dialogue around some of our society's greatest struggles.

One of the defining moments for me came after 9/11, to see how so many comic book writers approached the subject. Much of that had to do with the fact that many comic book characters are based in New York City, or some version of it. So they were deeply impacted by the attack. And knowing how deeply the country was affected, the writers and storytellers used the opportunity to unite the country. There have been great stories since then: some epic tales, and some smaller arcs that have been created that are just breathtaking and thought-provoking, and that when taken as a whole can really move the needle in our lives.

But the thing that really excites me is the origin story. So many comic book tales are being translated into movies and television today, and in my opinion the most successful ones are those with a great origin story. Adaptations that jump directly into the story are choppy; the next thing you know, there's a villain, then a chase, and a struggle, and it seems disoriented. I struggle with those movies and TV shows.

To devise a really good origin story and express it is what makes for a work of art in this genre. In my opinion, one of the best origin stories created recently would be Marvel's Netflix series version of Daredevil. I want to deconstruct that series a bit to create a formula for you to use in developing your own personal origin story.

Now, if the idea of an origin story is unfamiliar to you, let me explain briefly. An origin story is really the beginning. It's the tale of how the hero, superhero, or villain was created. An origin story is a way for readers to connect with the character. There are elements to this concept that can help you create your own origin story.

The journey of the dreamer is all making a dream happen. It's about taking something from our head and our heart, putting it into action and making it a reality. It is also all about the dreamer becoming the best version of themselves. The dreamer becomes the hero. The dreamer creates his or her own origin story.

In this last chapter I want to talk about your own origin story, and how you can become the hero of your own journey, the hero of your own epic tale. Let's drill down on this concept and bring it home. The origin story essentially has five key elements:

- Back story
- Internal conflict
- Villain
- Moment of truth
- First battle

Following the origin story, character development has to happen, and an ongoing story. And this to me is where many storytellers drop the ball. They can create a great origin story, but can they keep that story going? Can they develop the characters through the movies, or through the comics, through the TV series? Can they keep the character growing and developing in a way that's authentic, real and genuine, in a way that speaks to our hearts? To me, that's character development; that is the hero's journey. That's everything we've talked about so far in this book.

I encourage you to take some time, as you embark on or continue your own journey, to create your origin story. Create the story others will tell about you for generations and generations. While I know that sounds a bit dramatic, it can happen. Think about your kids, or your nieces and nephews, others who are close to you. You have the opportunity to impact the stories they tell about you, and how your life changed, and how you became a better version of yourself, and how you were driven by mission, and driven by passion and purpose. You have the opportunity to draft that story by considering these five elements of the origin story, how they relate to your life, and what they mean, and how they are tied together in your origin story.

First, the back story. All of us have a history. Some of us look at our back story as a negative thing, and maybe it is. You may have done things that you deeply regret. Things may have been done to you that are horrific. But the reality is, we can't go back and change that. Many of us spend our lives fighting our back story, trying to forget it, erase it, run from it. We go to counseling, psychologists, psychiatrists, to get wisdom or input or medication to help us to move past our back story.

Some of us self-medicate with addictions to alcohol or drugs or food. And some of us are just constantly running because we're trying to outperform our back story. We're trying to overcome our history so badly that we'll do whatever we have to do to make that happen. So we become overachievers. We set standards that nobody could ever live up to. We hold people to higher expectations than they can possibly imagine or fathom. We spend so much time fighting our back story. But what if the back story, your past, was actually a blessing?

I would like to encourage you ... actually, let me scratch that. I *dare* you to flip the script on your back story. Flip the script on your past. Flip the script on your history. Instead of looking at it as a negative, I dare you to look at it as a positive. And I know, for some, that's going to be incredibly difficult. You don't know my back story; you don't know the things I've done or the things that have been done to me. But I'm telling you, if you make the time and effort to flip the script, your history can become a beautiful part of your present and your future.

It may take counseling. It may take some therapy. It may take medication. It may take reaching out and asking for help. I'm begging you to do whatever it takes to make that a reality. I have had to do all of those. I have had medication at times, to help me overcome some of the things in my past. I have gone to counseling. I've gone to therapy. I've been a part of support groups. I have talked to many people, at many points in my life, about my past struggles, and I have come to a place where I believe I have overcome my past. I have not just accepted it, not just tolerated it, but embraced it as a beautiful and integral part of my story, one that has set me up for the present that I have, and the future that I will have.

Take some time right now to do an inventory of your life. I dare you to map out all of the negative things that have happened to you. All of the things people have done. All of the things people have said. Any time anybody has hurt you, or you have hurt them in any way, shape, or form—write it out. Work it out. Get real with it. Face it. Work through it.

Again, it may stir up a whole lot of emotion for you. For some, this may be incredibly difficult. For some, this may be the breaking point. You may put this book down right now and decide that you're never going to pick it up again. You may throw this entire concept out the window because of what I'm saying right now. But I dare you to flip the script on your back story.

Now I want you to take the time to write out all the positive things, those done to you, those you have done to others. For some people, this is the most difficult step, because we don't really want to admit when we've done things right. We don't own the positive areas of our lives. But it's important to put those two things together. That creates and rounds out your back story, giving the full picture of who you are and what you're about.

Once you've written it all out, the negative and the positive, take some time to ask the question I love, which is: "What can I learn from this, and how can I apply that learning to my life?"

Maybe you didn't learn from all this in the past, but the learning is happening right now. Maybe there are actions you need to take, words you need to say, conversations you need to have. Maybe that's part of the learning for you.

Take the time to do that now, and learn from the past so that you can apply it to the present and impact your future. That is the back story. Think about your favorite comic book character, or your favorite character in general. Everyone has a back story. Not all of them are positive. Not all of them are negative. But they are what they are. I dare you and invite you to stop running from your back story and instead embrace it as a part of your life, a part of your reality that is crucial for your character development and for your journey.

Now let's talk about the next element of the origin story, which is the internal conflict in the life of the hero. In every origin story there's an internal conflict. Typically, it's because the person who is to become the hero is struggling with who they are, what is happening around them, and what they hold dear.

Often the hero struggles with what is taking place in a society or culture. Bruce Wayne had a heart for Gotham City, so he became Batman. Mike Murdock had a heart for Hell's Kitchen and for the injustice happening there because he was an attorney, and so Daredevil was created.

Many other back stories are similar. Tony Stark had a business selling weapons and saw how those weapons were being used as war machines rather than to keep the peace, so he became Iron Man. Many back stories have this internal conflict between who the character is and what he holds dear, between the ideal world and the reality the hero sees.

Your own back story has helped to shape and mold you into the person that you are. If you were abused at one point in your life, then children growing up in abused homes may be a place of conflict for you—an internal struggle, something you see around you that you just can't stand to look at because it's too near and dear to your heart.

If you have been through a brutal divorce, maybe a marriage class or seeing couples going through marriage counseling or divorce presents an internal struggle for you. Maybe if you were in the military or saw a tragic event or experienced some turmoil in your life, again, all of these elements, all of these components of your back story, helped shape you.

You've set a standard for an ideal world that could exist outside of that reality. In your mind, you created an ideology that exists outside of that turmoil and of those circumstances, and the conflict begins to arise within you, a craving for something more, something greater.

Often when this conflict arises, you talk about it with others, dream about it and think about it. It may be easy to do so in the society that we live in because the conflict you feel is so prevalent. It's easy to take a step back and assume *I can't do anything about this* or *What is one person going to do?* or *It's silly to think that I can stop this because it's been happening forever.*

I want to challenge that thinking. I want you to stop for a moment and think of the moments in history where ideologies were disrupted or changed because of one person. Think of Dr. Martin Luther King. Of Rosa Parks. Think of the Founding Fathers. Think of the men and women who have given their lives for the freedoms that we have in this country. Think of the tragedies that have taken place that have spurred on movements and organizations to stop it: trafficking, starvation, suicides. Every organization and movement started with one person saying, "Enough is enough."

What could you do? What conflict is taking place within you? How can this conflict be joined with your back story and other elements of your origin story to create something amazing?

Take a moment now and spend some time writing down the internal conflict that takes place within your head and your heart every day. Take some time to list the areas where you find the most conflict. Compare that list to your back story, to see how those two things mesh to create something beautiful. See how your origin story is becoming more alive and vibrant because of the conflict present within it, because of the turmoil you've been through.

So many times we try to separate these historical experiences out and label them in categories of good or bad. I am asking you to take time to look at your past as neither good nor bad but just reality, and to consider how you can turn that reality from your past into a reality in your present and a reality in your future.

The next element of the origin story is the villain. Within that internal conflict, happening within the soul, the villain often appears. Many times in the origin stories we're used to, the villain is encapsulated in one person. That may be the case for you, but let's take some creative liberties here. Maybe the villain isn't an individual at all, but an ideological system that goes against your grain or your core.

Let me give you an example. When I worked for Zappos, one of the things we would often talk about is our competition. Who is our competition? It was easy to make the competitor out to be another online marketing giant.

One day, my thinking shifted dramatically; I realized the "villain" wasn't another company as much as it was an ideology. Zappos is all about great customer service, and at the time that's who we were and what we wanted to be about. So our competition was actually an ideology, which was bad customer service.

We all know what it's like to be online and to have a bad customer service experience. We know what it's like to be in a store and have a bad customer service experience. At Zappos, the desire was to do everything that we could to provide the opposite of that. The enemy, the competition, the villain, wasn't another company. It was bad customer service.

I want you to think about that in your own life. Your internal conflict is taking place, which is opening the space for a villain. What is that villain? If not a person, what's the ideology, the thought process, the system, in place going against your grain that you can create this origin story around and compete against?

Make the villain personal, something you can stand against and defeat. The point is not that we want to spend a lot of negative energy in life standing against things, BUT that we understand the impact the "villain" is having on society at large. In fact, once you have the "villain" identified, I would invite you to then create a persona that is clear and concise and so much more powerful than a villain could ever be…and then go and take a stand against that!

The heroes in our stories became heroes when they tapped into their inner strength and took a stand for the things they valued abd loved, the things in life that truly mattered. Too many of us today are standing against things; we stand against this party, we stand against this religious group, this creed or belief system, gender, ideology, etc. Where has that gotten us? Wars. Conflict. Suffering. What if we all decided to tap into the strength within and stand for something great, powerful and meaningful? What would happen if your villain pointed out your passion and created a desire within you to live life…full-out and with absolute abandon? Who would you be? What would you do right now? That is why the "villain" is so important…I challenge you to discover your villain and in so doing discover your strength!

Now we're looking at the fourth piece of the origin story. This is the piece I love: self-discovery. This is that moment of truth every hero goes through, that moment when the back story comes in conflict with the inner conflict and the villain. All of a sudden the hero understands his or her strength. In that moment, he or she has a choice. In that moment, there is another internal battle. Now that I know why I'm here, now that I know the struggle, now that I understand the impact it has in my life and the lives of others, now that I know I can do something about it, do I act? Do I put on my uniform and go to work? Do I take up my strength and go to work? Do I tap into the power that I have to overcome the villain and go to work?

This is that moment when we take everything we've learned from the journey and apply it. Quite frankly, this is the moment when many heroes blow it. This is that point when the world is crying out, when humanity is crying out, when the circumstances of life are crying out for someone to come to the rescue. Rather than stepping up and stepping in, often the hero checks out because of fear, or doubt, or insecurities, and sometimes because of laziness. Often it's simply because he or she lacks the passion or courage to take the step. This is that moment where you need to look at your life, to really dig down deep and discover who you truly are, and then make it happen.

Okay, so we've looked at four areas of the origin story so far: the back story, the internal conflict, the villain, and the moment of truth. Now I want to turn this around, because this is where the story gets amazing. What separates good origin stories from great ones is the first battle.

Now, I know what you're thinking. If we aren't going to be at war with each other, but stand in love and unity as I just talked about, then how can there be a first battle? Well, I want you to flip your thinking about battles, and what a battle scene looks like.

Unfortunately, I know what most people stand against in their anger and distress, and I'm not saying that's not valid. But what if we flipped it around, and instead of fighting *against* something, we fought *for* something? And what if the fight wasn't violent, but passionate? What if the fight wasn't rooted in scarcity, but abundance? What if, instead of going after the hearts and minds of others, we realized that there was enough good to go around? What if we saw that there was enough joy to go around? What if we recognized that I can stand for my truth, my values, and my mission, and you can stand for yours, and that we can both come out on top?

See, I think we've gotten into the mindset over the years that says that it's all or nothing. That there is only one victor, and the rest are losers. The conversation is rarely about win-win, or abundance, or the fact that there's more than enough to go around. The truth is, the first battle doesn't have to mean raging against someone or something, but rather about raging in your heart *for* something. How awesome would it be to identify the things you love in life, and then take a stand for those things?

Understanding that everybody has their opinion and things they hold dear, we can stand in unity, shining a light on what is valuable to us. If we could flip the script and recognize that standing for something amazing is an even more powerful act than standing against something we don't agree with, I believe we could change our culture, our society, and our world. To me, that's the making of an amazing origin story.

So what's the point of the first fight if we're not going to fight against something? To me, the point is to show what the journey has done for the hero: the back story, the internal conflict, recognizing the villain, and discovering the hero's strengths and capabilities—it all comes together in that first battle.

And it happens because of that moment of truth in which the hero dies to him- or herself, to old ways of being, and to things held dear. It's the moment of re-creation, where you discover your strengths, your gifts, your abilities. In that moment, you decide what you're going to stand for, and move forward into the battle from your strength rather than from fear, insecurity and doubt; to move from convictions, passions and a wish to make the world a better place to a burning desire to stand for something amazing.

So my question would be this: Have you discovered your inner strength? Have you discovered your convictions, your passions, your values, your purpose, your reason for being? Have you unlocked those things within your heart, and do you live every day from a place of strength, and power, and conviction? My own origin story is wrought with emotional turmoil, baggage, a history of mistakes and pain, some of which I brought on others, some of which others brought on me. All of it very real, and all of it very discouraging.

But I'm discovering a strength I have within me to go and make the world a better place. I'm discovering that, for me, the villain is a world lacking love and compassion. I'm discovering that the strength I want to live from, the value that I want to add, is to bring love, unity, and perspective into the world. I know that may sound altruistic, even fluffy and lacking substance. But I want to challenge that thinking.

See, I'm on a renewed journey of faith, where I'm understanding that God is a God of love, and ultimately what he has called us to is to love God and love others. And my understanding is that my life needs to be a life of love. Where there's love, there is passion, and purpose, and conviction, and unity, and service, and humility. Where there is love there is a greater value placed on the other person than on oneself. Where there is love, the focus isn't on what separates us and tears us apart, but what brings us together, and what we can do to create a better world.

When I think about love, I think about it in terms of action, purpose, and meaning. Love doesn't mean pretending we don't have differences, or joining hands and singing "Kumbaya," as the cliché goes. It's not simply saying loving things without backing it up. When I think about love, I think about sacrifice, selflessness, and service. My desire is to fight for love, to stand for love, to find men and women around the world to lock arms with and create a sense of unity that drives us forward.

Let me take that back. My desire is to create a sense of unity that propels us forward. One of the greatest lessons I learned in life, I learned while I was in the Boy Scouts. When we went camping, we would look around before we left the campsite, challenged by the troop leader, my dad, to leave it in better condition than we'd found it. I've made that my mission in life. Whenever I go anywhere, my desire is to leave that place better than it was when I got there.

That's what I want to do—to leave this world in a better place than it was when I got here. I know that sounds ambitious, and even as I'm writing it now, it is completely overwhelming, but I believe that we can change the world one dream at a time, one dreamer at a time, as we shift our thinking and learn to see the world from a new perspective, tapping into our greatest selves every moment of every day.

So I wrap up this chapter as I wrap up this book, asking this question: What is your dream? And what are you doing about it?

I believe that this book has given you a framework to go take action. There are more tools and resources available to you to help with this, many of which I provide, many of which you can find in the open market. I'll end much the same way I began. I'm begging you: please take time to discover your dream, to go after your dream, and to become the greatest version of yourself in the process.

Take a moment and just consider any area of your life where you feel the call to greatness, you feel the cry to step up and step in. Really look within and discover the passion and the power that's there. If you don't, who will? If you don't step up into this role, who will? If this is your mission, your purpose, your passion, and you decide to walk away from it, who is going to stand in your place? Who will stand for your truth? I simply want to ask the question: What is an area of life that you need to step up into right now? Where do you need to demonstrate more courage than maybe you've ever demonstrated in your life? This is that moment of truth. Your dream life is out there. Your passion and purpose are waiting. Will you step up and step in? Will you become the hero of your journey?

Now is the time to focus on Beliefs and Behaviors:

Application Questions:
- Have I been shying away from my "origin story"? What could I do today to embrace my story more?
- What defining moments have you experienced in life? How can they help you become the hero of your Journey?
- How can your origin story drive you into the Extraordinary Life you desire?

Action Items:
- Interact with the Elements of the Origin Story:
  - Back Story
  - Internal Conflict
  - Villain
  - Moment of Truth
  - First Battle
- Consider the following:
  - Write quickly what comes to mind in each area
  - Put these statements in to a paragraph or two [Story Draft]
  - Craft your Origin Story

- Share your Origin Story

Bonus Chapter: Time to Take Risks

On a plane today, I read an amazing book that I wanted to weave into this book because I think some of the principles in it apply. The book, *Rejection Therapy*, is about Jia Jiang, a man who practiced 100 days of rejection. Basically, the idea was to go around looking for ways to make people tell him "no." He created a list of ideas and went out to give them a try. The first thing he did was ask a stranger for $100. Naturally, the guy didn't give him $100, but asked him why he wanted it. Jiang just took off running because he was afraid of the rejection.

What's interesting is that, the more he did this, the more he engaged with people in an effort to get them to say "no," the more he grew personally—and the more he found people sometimes saying yes to his requests. The growth Jia Jiang experienced happened in that he realized that "no" wasn't a rejection of who he was, but a rejection of that for which he was asking. He also discovered that often we don't have because we don't ask. The deeper he went into this "study," the more Jia Jiang found that the depth of the "ask" stirred within others a desire to join him on the journey by simply saying "yes." This was a fascinating sociological test, because he put himself into the middle of his study and managed to succeed in getting people to say yes to things he'd assumed they'd say no to. Strangely, the bigger his requests became, the more these successes happened. Rather than just going for 100 bucks, he was actually making requests of people that would make a solid difference in the lives of others.

I love this concept because I believe it applies to dreams, as well. I think for most of us, that fear of rejection is really similar to the fear of failure. In fact, I put on my Facebook page today that I wanted to challenge people to do a "52 in 52" list, meaning, as you recall, coming up with 52 things that you're going to do with the 52 weeks this year, and then making them happen. Somebody said, "Do I have to make 52 in 52? Can't I just do 12? Because in all likelihood, I won't get these things done."

That's the point. The point is is that we need to push ourselves, we need to set goals and standards that will drive us to change our behaviors and change our current way of living.

When I challenge you to make a list of 1,000 dreams or 101 dreams that you want to go after, the reason is that I want to challenge you to change the way you do things. Not all of these dreams have to be epic. Some can be very simple.

In fact, I encourage you to to start simply—and simply start—because I want you to take steps toward achieving your dreams, big and small. Jia Jiang writes that, as a kid growing up in China, he would walk through the snow, dreaming and imagining all kinds of crazy things he would do someday, and somewhere along the way, he stopped dreaming in that way.

All of us, if we're honest with ourselves, at some point have dared to dream.

By creating this dream list and going after each item on it, you're saying: *You know what? I'm going to go after my dream.* That's what the journey of the dreamer is all about: stepping out of your comfort zone and moving into a space of risk, of challenge, of trials, where we learn and grow and become the greatest versions of ourselves, to achieve the supreme happiness that comes through peace.

Closing Thoughts

So there you go! That is the Journey of the Dreamer. My hope and desire is that something stirred within you to engage with your dreams again. I believe that within each of us is a greatness that we have suppressed, ignored and avoided for far too long. It's time to get after it. It's time for each of us to step up, own our dreams, create a future that is greater than anything we could have ever imagined.

When I was a Boy Scout my Troop Leader, my dad, used to tell us to leave every campsite we entered in better shape than it was when we found it…something I still live by today. Why not apply this to our lives and to our world? We live in a world with such disarray, confusion and despair. We live in a world where people are searching for hope; the hope of a new and better life, the hope of a bright future, the hope that life has a great meaning that any of us could ever imagine!

Why can't WE be the answer for which others are searching?

I believe **The Journey of the Dreamer** can provide that hope as each of us begin to live into our greatest selves and leave this world in better shape than it was when we were born into it. I hope you sense my passion for this "hope" and that my passion stirs within your heart and soul to move each of you to greatness!

The Journey of the Dreamer Resource Guide:

Follow Donavon:

Facebook: facebook.com/donavon.roberson

JOTD Facebook Page: facebook.com/TheJourneyOfTheDreamer

Instagram: instagram.com/donavonroberson/

Twitter: twitter.com/donavonroberson

YouTube: youtube.com/donavonroberson

Contact Donavon:
donavon@thejourneyofthedreamer.com

The Journey of the Dreamer Worksheet and Companion Resources:

www.thejourneyofthedreamer.com/worksheets

Coaching, Speaking and Training:

Dream Coaching (Individual and Group Coaching)

Are you living your Dream Life? Most of us have achieved a few dreams but not those dreams that are deep within our hearts. If you are ready to take your life to the next level and make your dreams a reality…I am here for you!

Speaking Engagements

I am available to Speaking Engagements to small and large groups. If you have need of a speaker to inspire and motivate an audience to dream big and take action, I would love to connect with you on making that a reality!

Training Sessions

I have developed 1 and 2 Day Packages where we can take a team through The Journey of the Dreamer and inspire those in attendance to take massive action! This training can be for teams of any size and within any organization and can be customized to meet your needs.

About Donavon

Donavon has been coaching people in a variety of settings for nearly 20 years and desires to help reconnect people with what makes them great, so that they have massive impact in their world. He takes the approach of discovering where they are in their life, where they would truly like to be and then come up with a strategic plan to become the greatest version of themselves.

Donavon's experience ranges from ministry to small and medium sized business consulting. He approaches Dream Coaching and Business Coaching as he would in helping a small business succeed; vision, mission, monthly - weekly - daily goals and both personal and leadership development. His belief is that if you're going to be successful in life, you need to approach it AS the owner of your life! As a speaker, trainer and coach he draws upon his experience as small business consultant and utilize the areas below to help create success!

This experience has come from working in such companies as Zappos, Infusionsoft, Dyn, Origami Owl and Isagenix where he took a hands on approach at keeping leaders and employees engaged and performing at high levels. He created powerful training programs (content and curriculum) in several of these companies including; Zappos – Zappos Insights, Infusionsoft – Employee Dream

Program, Isagenix – Step Up to Success and Step Up to 2 Star Training. Many of these programs are still active and effective today.

Donavon was enlisted in the Air National Guard for 6 years, served as a Pastor of Youth Ministries for nearly 13 years and has had the opportunity to speak publicly in a variety of settings. He and his wife Anjie have 6 kids between them, 2 dogs and currently live in Chandler, AZ with dreams of one day living in Scotland!

Made in the USA
Columbia, SC
27 August 2018